W9-BPK-718

FOCUS ON THE FAMILY®

Why A.D.H.D. Doesn't Mean Disaster

FOCUS ON THE FAMILY®

Why A.D.H.D. Doesn't Mean Disaster

TYNDALE

Tyndale House Publishers, Inc.
Wheaton, Illinois

Dennis Swanberg & Diane Passno
with medical contributions by **Walt Larimore, M.D.**

Why ADHD Doesn't Mean Disaster
Copyright © 2003 by Dennis Swanberg, Diane Passno,
and Walter L. Larimore, M.D.
All rights reserved. International copyright secured.

ISBN: 1-58997-127-2

A Focus on the Family book published by
Tyndale House Publishers, Wheaton, Illinois 60189

Focus on the Family books are available at special quantity discounts
when purchased in bulk by corporations, organizations, churches, or
groups. Special imprints, messages, and excerpts can be produced to
meet your needs. For more information, contact: Resource Sales
Group, Focus on the Family, 8605 Explorer Drive, Colorado Springs,
CO 80920; or phone (800) 932-9123.

Library of Congress Cataloging-in-Publication Data
Swanberg, Dennis, 1953-
 Why ADHD doesn't mean disaster / Dennis Swanberg, Diane
Passno; with medical contributions by Walter L. Larimore, M.D.
     p. cm.
"A Focus on the Family book."
Includes bibliographical references.
  ISBN 1-58997-127-2
1. Attention-deficit hyperactivity disorder—Popular works.
I. Passno, Diane. II. Larimore, Walter L. III. Title.
RJ506.H9 S93 2003
618.92'8589—dc21

                                                    2003001351

Editors: Mick Silva and Kathy Davis
Cover Design: Kurt Birky
Copy Writer: Joy Olson
Cover Photos: Mark Waters

Printed in the United States of America
1 2 3 4 5 6 7 8 9 / 09 08 07 06 05 04 03

*Lovingly dedicated to Chad Swanberg and Nicole Passno
for their exemplary behavior in loving and leading
the way for their ADHD brother and sister.
Your parents could not have survived without you!*

———————

Table of Contents

Contents

ADHD: A Dividend—Not a Disaster

*Several elements of the ADD mind favor creativity . . .
the term "attention deficit" is a misnomer. It is a matter
of attention inconsistency. While it is true that the ADD
mind wanders when it is not engaged, it is also the case
that the ADD mind fastens on to its subject fiercely
when it is engaged. A child with ADD may sit for hours
meticulously putting together a model airplane.*
—EDWARD HALLOWELL, M.D. and JOHN RATEY, M.D.[1]

Once upon a time there were two old ladies who lived in a
shabby little house near a railroad switchyard. At one time,
the living room with its big picture window had been their
favorite place to sit. However, the view from their window
had become increasingly depressing over the years. No matter how hard they tried to keep the window clean, it was
always dirty from the activity in the train yard.

One day, they hired a skilled artist to paint a forest land-
scape over the glass. When he had finished, the afternoon

light shone through the window on a beautiful woodland scene. The living room had become more beautiful than ever! And the two old women had a brand new perspective on life.

Parents of ADHD kids need much the same thing. Yet far from simply "painting over" the challenges of ADHD, many parents could use a completely new perspective about their children. We would all like to have the "don't-rock-the-boat" kid; we don't want our lives in constant turmoil. But as with many things in life, the more effort that's required, the more rewarding the successes will be. In order to get that new perspective, we desperately need to see the benefits and to tap into the dividends of ADHD's unique characteristics.

The last thing in the world parents want to learn is that their beloved little bundle of joy has a prognosis that might limit his opportunities, particularly when he's just starting out. The stereotype ADHD has given to these kids is simply awful. And most parents lack either the understanding or the confidence to challenge the conventional thinking. There is a lot of hype surrounding this issue. Is it a real condition? Aren't ADHD kids just unruly, undisciplined, or unloved? Shouldn't we just stop feeding them so much sugar and expect them to pay attention in class? Is this all part of some conspiracy to drug children into submission?

The truth is out there. Every parent knows that stereotyping kids is dangerous and deceptive. It can do unseen damage to a child's understanding of who he is and what he is able to accomplish in life. As early as kindergarten, if a child is told that he has a mental disability and he begins to feel he is destined to fail, he will begin to live up to the expectation. He will become the classic underachiever. And as these kids become teenagers, their lack of self-respect can take on a desperate quality, putting them at risk for undesirable behaviors such as substance abuse or even suicidal feelings. Finding the hope behind the mask of ADHD is imperative.

Diane has a goldfish that will probably outlive everyone in her family. This 29-cent prize had been in a bowl on the kitchen sink for the past six years, swimming around and around in a tight little circle. One day, she moved Sgt. Pepper to a huge tank, six times the size of his old domain. For the first several days, he continued to swim in the same tight little circles the size of his old bowl. He didn't understand that his world had expanded. In a similar way, a child who becomes "that ADHD kid who drives everyone nuts" may never understand what he can accomplish with his unique set of gifts. And if he is never given permission to be anything different, most likely he never will.

Well, that's why we think it's time to expand the bowl in which ADHD kids have been placed. In the following chapters, we want to offer:

- encouragement for you, your family, and your child or children diagnosed with ADHD;
- the positive side of ADHD—the gifts and abilities of these uniquely created people; and
- a new perspective for any of you—parents, caregivers, and educators—who have the privilege—that's right, the *privilege*—of having an ADHD kid in your life.

Walt is a physician. Diane and I (Dennis) are parents of ADHD kids. And I've had ADHD all my life, so I also speak from firsthand experience.

This book has been a particular passion of mine for years. It has been my privilege, first in the pulpit, and later as a public speaker with my own television program, to overcome the barriers ADHD poses and find the benefits. None of these successes were even on my radar screen when I was young and struggling simply to get through another day at school. But if I can make it, anyone can. I hope to encourage those of you who are having similar difficulties raising a kid like I once was.

Even so, our main purpose for writing this book is to

encourage you and help you consider that Attention Deficit Hyperactivity Disorder can be a *dividend* rather than a disease or mental disability. It can be turned into a blessing rather than a curse, an asset rather than a handicap. Sure, there will always be challenges and frustrations associated with something out of the ordinary like ADHD. But by the time you finish this book, we hope and pray that no matter whether you have ADHD yourself, or are the parent of an ADHD child, you will see your future from a hopeful new perspective.

2

All about Dennis

Impulsivity . . . spontaneity, little tolerance for boredom,
in addition to daydreaming, are listed as identifying
characteristics of creative individuals. . . . Given that
some highly creative children engage in "disruptive,
attention-seeking behavior" in the classroom, it is not
surprising that they are not valued by their teachers as
much as more conforming, less creative students.
—BONNIE CRAMOND, PH.D.[1]

When I was a kid, I loved to listen to the radio, watch TV, or take in a movie—*anything* rather than read a book. I wanted to see action, feel it, smell it, and handle it! That was much more exciting than sitting and trying to comprehend words on a page. I loved to play cowboys and Indians, especially with my toy soldiers. I was a huge Roy Rogers and Dale Evans fan, and I would relive their episodes in my backyard, adding a few lines of dialogue myself. I could entertain myself for hours this way.

The Wizard of Oz was my favorite movie, and I would imitate the characters by putting myself in their shoes. I made up my own scripts in which I imagined myself dealing with their difficulties and accomplishments. I loved acting out all the parts, even though I was an audience of one.

I had a big imagination. Every season of the calendar year was embellished in my fantasy world. Christmas and Easter were especially wonderful. Maybe that's why I became a pastor. I was always able to understand the thrill and mystery of what God accomplished on those days.

My favorite thing to do was listen to stories from the older folks in my family. Everything for me had a story line—the truth or lesson I could hang my hat on forever. I would sit on the floor by the old folks at reunions and listen to them talk about their experiences, struggles, and achievements. I was enthralled. In hindsight, if the same stories had been in book form, I never would have read them. It was the hearing of the stories that held me captive.

Even now, over 40 years later, I can recall stories told by my daddy and my grandpa. My favorite story was about two boys named Piggy and Hoggy who lived with their disabled parents in an abandoned boxcar. The two boys would walk to the main highway to sell peanuts. An old cardboard box served as their stand, and they made just enough money to make ends meet.

One day, a traveling evangelist stopped and bought some peanuts. The preacher invited them to a revival that evening, but the boys declined, embarrassed that they had no church clothes to wear. The preacher nodded and took them across the highway and bought them each a pair of jeans, shirts, and coats and ties—the first new clothes they had ever owned. The preacher even offered to give them a ride to the meeting.

When they got to the tent meeting that evening, the boys were so captured by the Bible stories they sat riveted to their seats, and at the conclusion they gave their lives to Jesus. The local pastor offered his church for the traveling evangelist to baptize the new converts the following week.

Years passed and the evangelist returned to hold another revival meeting. During the two decades he was away, he'd become a successful senior pastor of a large congregation in a big city back East. But he still loved the tent meetings in smaller towns. The pastor of the local church had changed since he had been there last, but the church had grown, and the traveling evangelist was treated to a tour by the new pastor.

The evangelist couldn't get over how much the old church had grown. In one of the packed Sunday school classes, the evangelist asked to meet the teacher, a young man who was obviously enjoying his ministry.

"Don't you remember me?" the Sunday school teacher asked.

The evangelist frowned.

"I'm Piggy!" exclaimed the young man.

Well, the old evangelist couldn't believe it! Tears flowed down his wrinkled face. He'd thought about the two boys he'd baptized many times over the years and prayed for them. Piggy's enthusiasm for the gospel was greater than he could have ever imagined. During the days that followed, the evangelist learned that Hoggy had become a preacher as well. The Lord had shown the evangelist the visible results of his labor, and he returned to his own congregation with renewed enthusiasm for his work.

Now, you might think that's a pretty hokey story. But I used to ask my daddy to tell it time and again. Deep down, I wanted to be that kind of man, someone who could help others, someone with a life-changing touch. I still identify with Piggy and Hoggy because I've known a lot of people like that old evangelist who have helped me through the years. Even as a young boy, I knew what it was like to be the recipient of kindness. And who knows? Maybe that story was the beginning of my own journey to becoming a pastor.

When I entered grade school, I was always more interested in friendships than in reading and writing. I was thrilled to have 24 new friends because now I had a captive audience to entertain! It was my goal to make sure everybody in class had FUN, FUN, FUN! I would act like I was the Lone Ranger, or I would imitate TV characters—Paul Lynde, Don Knotts, and Andy Griffith. At recess I would imitate television sports announcers. I learned all the facial expressions, and early on I learned that I could make people laugh—especially when I imitated the teacher and the principal.

It was inevitable I guess: The class was so busy watching me that my teacher did something that first year of school that was repeated every year, even through graduate school. My teachers always said, "You're going to be my helper and sit right next to my desk!" After that, the audience was always behind me. I decided that the only way to make it in school was to woo my teachers. I knew I was a tough one to handle, but I could make them laugh! And even though they

---

Dr. Larimore: Allen's mother brought him to my office because he was failing second grade. His IQ testing was, according to her, "off the chart." Yet, because of his easy distractibility, he was frequently berated by his classmates and his teacher as a goof-off. His principal wondered aloud to Allen's mother if he wasn't doomed to be an "anarchist"—one who simply refused to follow the rules. Because of this intensely negative feedback from educators and students, Allen had incredibly low self-esteem. He withdrew and began to keep to himself. As a result he had few friends.

I smiled to myself as Allen's mother told me the story. Not only was I fairly certain of the diagnosis, but I knew I could give her and her son help and hope.

Allen fidgeted in the corner chair. I rolled my chair over to him and began to ask him a series of questions. Then I did a brief exam, ordered some lab work, and gave Allen's mom a questionnaire for herself and her husband and another for his teacher. When all the studies were

always wrote on my report card, "Talks too much," in many ways I knew I was refreshing to them. Once in a while I'd have to pay the price and sit in the corner, or go to the principal's office, or do extra laps for a coach, even though they were laughing. I didn't fit their mold, but I made them laugh.

I was the life of the party, but I wasn't cutting it in school. In elementary school, I wanted to be first: the first to finish the test, the first to read through a book. But my answers were not always correct, and I didn't understand what I had read by the time I finished. I couldn't seem to concentrate long enough to comprehend anything. I would daydream. I would become interested in the room, the ceiling, the activities outside the window, or the ballgame I was to play that night at the park.

I think the turning point in my life occurred in the third

---

completed, we had our diagnosis. He clearly and unequivocally met the diagnostic criteria for ADHD.

We talked about all of the available treatment options, both standard and alternative. Allen and his mom chose a trial of medication and agreed to some family counseling. With the help of the counseling, Allen's parents and siblings learned how to appreciate his unique giftedness and found more effective ways to communicate with him.

Medication dramatically helped Allen concentrate in the classroom. His parents and teacher were able to negotiate a number of highly effective changes. Allen's mom said, "It was like the family, the counselors, the teacher, and the school all had to learn about Allen's unique wiring. We learned from each other, taught each other—and we were all beneficiaries of the effort."

"Was it worth the cost and time?" I asked.

She smiled as she thought about how to frame her response. "My child is worth every moment, every struggle, every cent."

---

grade. The entire class took a series of achievement tests to see how we compared with other students in the state. I can still remember the anguish of that ordeal. My teacher announced to the class, "Dennis Swanberg didn't do very well." I made a joke out of it, but deep down, it hurt. I began to wonder whether I was retarded or just plain dumb. Was I truly different from other kids? Did I belong in Special Ed?

By the time third grade rolls around, the cream is beginning to rise to the top. The brains of the class are revealed, and every kid knows where he or she stands. Kids begin to label each other as smart or dumb. I found my self-image beginning to crumble, and life seemed a lot more complicated than it had ever been before.

It was in third grade that I started to become "street

Dr. Larimore: Many ADHD children will have difficulty finishing tasks or remembering details, focusing on a book or assignment, or even remaining seated for more than a few minutes. Although this lack of concentration is often seen as a problem, the opposite side of the coin is often unrecognized: these kids usually have the special ability of what ADHD experts call "multiple-track cognition." They have a much higher awareness of their surroundings and environment. They can both see and recall details that their non-ADHD peers completely miss.

Adolescents and even adults with ADHD are at increased risk for job and relationship failures. Some with ADHD appear to be driven from within as they race wildly from one thing to another. They are usually very bright and creative, yet many uninformed observers view them as lazy, disruptive, and terribly disorganized. They mentally process a multitude of thoughts simultaneously. To a logical thinker, ADHD thinking may seem jumbled and disorganized. But even though the conclusions of the ADHD individual may seem illogical, they can be unusually creative—even groundbreaking.

smart" to compensate. I used humor to cover the pain I was feeling about being different from the other kids. Matthew 10:16 says, "be as shrewd as snakes and as innocent as doves," and now that I look back, I think that describes me at that time of my life. I had to develop the cleverness to get around the "minefields" in the academic classroom every day, but do it without injuring anybody else's feelings.

I learned to intentionally get to know my teachers and make sure they knew me. I would talk to them before and after class, visit with them during their office hours, and ask them for help when I was really stumped. If I felt they liked me, I would work all the harder just to please them. They would often give me the benefit of the doubt when I struggled with an answer in class because they knew how hard I was working. They wanted me to succeed because I had taken the time to nurture a relationship.

I found that I could really shine in subjects like English and journalism if the teacher allowed me to give a verbal rather than a written report. I covered all the same material when I gave the report, but I didn't have to struggle to get it down on paper. I got great grades when they let me do this because I'd add humor to get the point across. The result was that my reports were really entertaining, rather than just informative or factual.

When I gave a verbal report, the teacher and the class were so entertained that I suddenly felt like a winner rather than a loser. And my image began to change: My friends started to think that maybe I wasn't the dummy they'd thought I was. To this day, I use the same technique I did back then to prepare for a performance: I tape-record what I want to say, transcribe it, and then make changes to the routine as I study the result.

Another way I got around the minefields in the classroom was doing the exact opposite of what they tell you to do in business management seminars: I would do all the little

Why ADHD Doesn't Mean Disaster

things first—knock out all the small things cluttering up my desk. This freed my mind to do the big things without any distractions. Also, I would not study for an exam until the night before a test because I learned that I would forget the material if I prepared too far in advance. Again, this is probably the opposite of what a student without ADHD would do, but I was fighting to survive in school!

No one knew how badly I was hurting inside because of my struggle to survive in school. I didn't think my parents would understand. My conduct in school seemed to be more important to them than my education. I felt very much alone a lot of the time, and I didn't know anybody to turn to for encouragement or emotional support. I guess I could have shared some of these feelings with a few of my favorite teachers, but I shoved them all inside, and it wasn't until my own son was tested for ADHD years later that I was finally able

---

Dr. Larimore: Les Linet, M.D., a psychiatrist at the Beth Israel Medical Center in New York City, has written, "If I was in charge of renaming ADHD—and I'm not—I would call it 'search for stimulation' disorder."[2] She goes on to point out, speaking of a young boy (Timmy) with ADHD, "Just as nature hates a vacuum, so, too, [his] nervous system hates sensory deprivation. So, if Timmy doesn't get stimulation, he will seek it out. This would explain Timmy's excessive need or, perhaps better put, his thirst for any stimulating information or event. Timmy wants to do well. He wants to make his parents proud of him. But he just can't seem to do this, because of his excessive need for stimulation."

At the most basic level, those with ADHD have difficulty with regulation of focus and attention. So that means they can be very underfocused at times, when the tasks are boring or repetitive. When their brains are really connected with what they're doing, they're overfocused. They easily flip-flop back and forth.

to express the pain I had kept hidden for so long. (But that's a story for a later chapter.)

If I'd had a tutor, it would have been a godsend. But I didn't, so I just began to float through the system, filling in the gaps with humor and sports. ADHD wasn't even in the vocabulary back then, and I think everybody just thought of me as a goof-off. They didn't know how much I ached inside, how much it bothered me that I wasn't like everybody else in the classroom. Why did academics come so easily to them and not to me? I studied and worked harder than any of my friends, and I was just not making it!

I did just well enough to be passed on to middle school, but the English, math, and science courses were tough for me. Again, I learned "the system," put my personality into overdrive, and made it work. But by the time I got to high school, I could no longer hide my weaknesses. I decided that anyone as stupid as I was couldn't go to college, so I took courses for the non college-bound students.

The funny thing is, even though I was struggling with all this internal turmoil, the tactics I used to survive paid off! I was a class officer; I helped start a chapter of Fellowship of Christian Athletes at my school; I was a Rotary honorary Youth of the Month winner as well as a Kiwanis Award Teenager and an Optimist Club Youth Award winner! And I was asked to speak and perform all the time!

I will never forget the night of our football banquet after our team had won the Texas State Football Championship in 1970. The Lt. Governor of Texas was there to speak, but the coach asked me to say a few words to the audience beforehand. I did a whole handful of imitations of entertainers popular at that time and even included an imitation of the head coach. The audience howled, and the headlines in the newspaper the next day read, "Swanberg Steals Show!" My ADHD was the reason I could get up and entertain a crowd.

However, athletics was really what saved me. I played

football and baseball and was All District in both sports. I would never have had the opportunity for the success I enjoy today if a football scholarship hadn't gotten me into college. I could never have become a pastor or a speaker or have had a successful television show if it had not been for that athletic scholarship!

God had a plan for my life. But sometimes, late at night when sleep eludes me on the road, I hang my head in my hands and wonder what would have become of the ol' Swan if I had been uncoordinated and never set foot on an athletic field. The academic system would have doomed me, and it's very likely I would not have lived up to my potential or been able to use the gifts God gave me to help others.

In the next chapter, we'll hear from Diane and her daughter Danielle who was diagnosed with ADHD in college.

Lessons Learned

1. Overactive kids may have untapped creativity.
2. Underachieving may be a mask ADHD children wear.
3. Some ADHD kids learn to cope in school by becoming "street smart" and learning the system. It is their way to survive in a "hostile" environment.
4. Although ADHD kids often have the tendency to become underachievers, they may put in longer hours and work harder than other students.

Reflection

Diane: In the next chapter, you will read about my daughter Danielle. But one memory in particular stands out from when she was in the first grade. Her teacher tried to tell me about Danielle's inability to understand verbal directions. "She asks way too many questions about every assignment. It's wearing me out!" Since this particular teacher was new to the school and always looked frazzled, I decided—somewhat stupidly in hindsight—that it was her problem rather than Danielle's. I never bothered to dig any deeper, never even talked about it with Danielle.

Questions for Parents

Have you had a good talk with your child lately, eyeball to eyeball? Do you know what is really going on in his head, how he really feels about his teacher, his school, and his friends? Have you assured him that you are a safe confidant? Does your child understand that you care about the trouble he is having in school, both academically and socially, and that God is in the business of answering prayers? Does your child know how much God loves children?

> *When I am afraid, I will trust in you. In God, whose word I praise, in God I trust; I will not be afraid. What can mortal man do to me? ... Record my lament; list my tears on your scroll—are they not in your record? Then my enemies will turn back when I call for help. By this I will know that God is for me. In God, whose word I praise, in the LORD, whose word I praise—in God I trust; I will not be afraid. What can man do to me?* (Psalm 56:3-4; 8-11)

3

All about Danielle

Being ADD, when I read a book about marine life my mind allows me to travel with the fish and imagine life beneath the sea. Or I can read a book about astronomy and dance among the stars. . . . I may not immediately comprehend that 3+4=7, but I may fully realize that n+26=51 and that the missing number is 25.
—MATTHEW KUTZ, age 13[1]

Diane: Danielle was always different. Moments after birth, when the obstetrician put her to my breast to nurse, my husband, Paul, and I chuckled at the exuberance she showed about attacking her first meal!

I used to laughingly say to Danielle that if she had been born first, rather than her sister, we would have not had any more children. However, there is a grain of truth in every joke, and the truth in this case is that Paul and I would never have had the energy to endure another toddler stage! We barely survived that one.

I had a difficult pregnancy with Danielle, and I have since learned that what I went through is not unusual for mothers who deliver children diagnosed with ADHD. My prenatal care was relegated to the "complicated pregnancy" unit of our PPO, and I saw the resident obstetrician weekly.

During the course of those visits, I had one incident that secretly terrified me. It happened during an ultrasound procedure, when I overheard the technician say to the nurse, "The brain is not developing as it should."

At the time, I was attending a Bible study where I was the youngest member. When I told the dear, older women in the study about my fears regarding my baby's brain development, they began to pray for her at the conclusion of every meeting. I believe with all my heart that our daughter is a direct answer to their prayers, for when she was born, her body was healthy and her brain was fully developed. And she was incredibly alert. If she could have talked, she would have shouted, "Hello, world! Here I am! Get excited!" I have always thought of her as God's miracle.

Are the brains of people with ADHD different?

Dr. Larimore: Although the cause of ADHD is unknown, the theories abound. Some believe it is associated with subtle differences in brain structure. Brain scans reveal a number of subtle changes in the brains of those diagnosed with ADHD. In fact, one of the former names used for ADHD was "minimal brain disorder."

Others say it's related to neural pathways, neurotransmitters, or brain chemistry—particularly abnormalities in the brain chemical dopamine. Still other researchers believe ADHD is related to the brain's blood supply or electrical system. Recent research has raised the question of whether frequent exposure in early childhood to rapid electronic stimuli (such as television and computers) might contribute to this problem.

Richard DeGrandpre, in his book *Ritalin Nation: Rapid-fire Culture and the Transformation of Human Consciousness*,[2] theorizes about what he calls a "sensory addiction phenomenon." He feels that many of the behaviors seen in ADHD people stem from a sensory bombard-

All about Danielle

I guess I was like every other mother of a newborn in that I had so many expectations for this precious child. So I simply ignored the volume of signals that Danielle was not the average kid. She never napped as an infant, but since I was an extremely active person myself, I accepted this as an advantage. Danielle was always cheerful and seldom cranky, so she was a pleasure to have around, even if she didn't sleep!

However, when she was about one year old, her activity ruined what was supposed to be a restful camping trip. Forget the playpen—that wasn't for her! Danielle toddled around our big campground, with her sister, her dad, and me taking turns in pursuit. She walked and walked and walked, hour after hour, until we were all at each other's throats from

---

ment from TV programs, movies, computers, and so on. He feels that early exposure to this sensory bombardment, especially at a time when the brain is just forming connections and synapses, may result in biological or neurological effects, including, but not limited to, ADHD.

DeGrandpre believes that these effects can be exaggerated in the absence of parental structure. We live in a world that is incredibly stimulating; there are constant stimuli in the life of even a very young child. I don't know that we can really get rid of all that, but I know that we can encourage parents to provide a loving, warm, structured environment so children can learn to deal with all of that stimuli with the help of parents.

One piece of data that may support DeGrandpre's theory is the experience of the Amish, who are known to forgo computers and television. This keeps their children from this type of stimulation, and ADHD appears to be uncommon among the Amish. Researchers have reported that among 200 Amish children followed prospectively and compared with the non-Amish population, symptoms of ADHD were unusual.[3]

exhaustion. I took her into the camper with me while I fixed dinner, but she wanted to continue to run in the great outdoors. Trying to escape, she leaned against what we thought was a childproof door. The door gave way, and Danielle executed a perfect one-and-a-half somersault out into the dirt! We thought this was surely only a freak accident, but within the next half hour, she managed to wreak havoc on the door twice more. When she bloodied her nose on the last descent, we cut the trip short and went home.

When our older daughter, Nicole, was eight years old, Paul took her on a Summit Adventure, a Christian outdoor camping and rapelling trip. Nicole thrived on this trip, but then, she would actually think before leaping off a cliff. Not Danielle. Her way of approaching any adventure was to throw her entire body into it, ignoring any danger and enduring the physical pain and broken bones that resulted. Convinced that Danielle would kill herself, my husband never exposed her to Summit Adventure. Instead, we directed her toward girls' sports, and that is where she excelled.

Sports afforded our daughter an avenue in which she could run and "punish" her body until she literally dropped from exhaustion. She loved it! We put her in every sports program we could find because this was a positive way to channel the abundant energy she possessed. We never considered her hyperactivity a problem that might require a physician's attention or medication. ADHD was not even on our radar screen.

When ADHD became a popular talk show subject, we brushed it off as simply another fad disorder. My husband, a college professor, thought of it as an overused reason to avoid responsibility . . . the excuse to end all excuses in order to obtain leniency on exams and homework. Besides, we thought ADHD was only for dummies, and our child was the high school valedictorian.

Danielle had a plethora of opportunities available to her

for college because of her scholastic and athletic abilities. She was named the All State shortstop in softball, and she played forward on a soccer team that either won the State Championship or was a finalist all four years she was in high school. The letters from wonderful institutions of higher learning filled a large packing box in our home office. They came so often, and in such abundance, that we simply didn't open them after a while. Danielle's selection was a surprise: She chose to go to an Ivy League college with no academic or athletic scholarships.

We didn't think it unusual that Danielle would have difficulty with some of the subject matter in college, and we prepared her not to expect the same grades she had achieved in high school. She told us several times that she was struggling, but we told her that getting B's and C's was not something to worry about. She also verbalized some concerns about her relationship with her college softball coach, but again, we brushed this off as part of the "freshman jitters."

We received a telephone call from our daughter during her sophomore year at Dartmouth. "Mom, I went to talk to my physics professor today. I can't understand why I'm having such a hard time in his class. He says that he has noticed some characteristics about my style of learning that may mean I'm ADHD, and that's why I'm having trouble. He thinks I should be tested for it!"

In my ignorance, I responded, "The guy must be nuts. High school valedictorians don't have learning disabilities! These Ivy League intellectual types always have to have a theory about why kids are not learning in their classes because it takes the criticism away from them as instructors. Ignore him! There is absolutely nothing wrong with you!"

Several weeks later, Danielle called again, "Mom, my professor is really encouraging me to go through testing. Do we have insurance that covers it? He says it's pretty expensive."

"But Honey, there isn't anything wrong with you. It's OK

not to get great grades in every class. Maybe physics just isn't your thing. The only reason those academic types want kids like you to be tested is to try out their educational theories on human guinea pigs!"

"But Mom, I really think he is trying to help me. He thinks I'll make a wonderful engineer because kids with this type of disability think outside of the box. He wants me to understand why I'm having trouble because he thinks it will help me deal with my frustration better."

Reluctantly, my husband and I agreed for Danielle to go ahead with the testing. I'm embarrassed to say that we completely forgot about this entire issue for several months, until a bill for the testing arrived in the mailbox. We called her for a report.

"Danielle! We just got the bill from the doctor who did your testing, but there aren't any results attached to it. What happened? Was it a complete waste of time?"

"Oh! I guess I forgot to tell you! The doctor says that I have ADHD/Combined Disorder with an unspecified auditory learning disorder."

"Honey! That's just gobbledygook to us. What does that mean?"

"Well, I scored at the highly superior level in my IQ testing, but I scored in the mental retardation level for auditory processing. It just means that I have trouble translating anything I hear into practice."

My husband and I were stunned to learn about Danielle's auditory problem. Suddenly, many things we had simply overlooked in her childhood surfaced for re-examination, including our own prejudices about people diagnosed with learning disabilities.

Danielle's Story

I always knew that I did more work and took longer to do it than everyone else when I was in high school. I thought it was because I had made my mind up to be class valedictorian, and working harder was the price I had to pay to achieve that. But when I went to college, I was at the same academic and intelligence level as every other entering freshman, and my studies still took me twice as long to do as everyone else. I began to suspect that maybe I did have some type of problem with learning information. My physics professor was the one who figured out something was wrong. In one way, I'm relieved to know why everything is so much more difficult for me, but in another way, it really hasn't made much difference.

I've always had a lot of energy, but I would never want to

Is ADHD different in boys and girls?

Dr. Larimore: It is important to realize that while ADHD is usually associated with hyperactivity, there is a form that is not. This form is especially common in girls, although obviously not all girls with ADHD. Girls with predominately inattentive type ADHD will usually be seen as dreamy or detached. Unfortunately, some will be called "airheads" or "space cadets." Such a young lady can look at a book for 30 minutes without reading a word.

One parent told me that their daughter would lose every article of clothing that wasn't hooked to her body. Nearly every day, this child's teacher would have to send her back to the playground to retrieve her sweater or coat, only to have her return 15 minutes later without it, having forgotten what she went after.

A boy or girl with that kind of distractibility would find it extremely difficult, if not impossible, to get home night after night with books and assignments written down, and then to complete the work and turn it in the next morning.

Dr. James Dobson has written, "Frankly, the 'far away' child worries me more than the one who is excessively active. She may be seen as a good little girl, who just isn't very bright, while the troublemaker is more likely to get the help he needs. He's too irritating to ignore."[4]

change that or the way my brain works. I know my thought process is different from other kids because what I'm thinking about a subject never matches what comes out of other people's mouths. It shows up all the time in class. Other students will think about a piece of literature in the same way

---

What is my child feeling?

Dr. Larimore: At Focus on the Family, we receive letters from children, adolescents, and young adults who live with ADHD. One of the most heartrending came from a boy in the seventh grade. Here's a portion of what he wrote:

> When I began the second grade, I went from having a good teacher to a hard one. I did not feel ready for second grade, and felt different from the other kids. Writing words were hard, like writing the Korean numbers. No letters or numbers made sense, and I had trouble remembering everything I learned. I did not understand and remember the directions, and everyone seemed mad at me all the time.
>
> When you're in the second grade . . . you really feel the pressure to wear cool clothes and hang out with cool friends and do good in school. I began to feel like I was a failure and heard my teacher tell my mom I was at the bottom of my class. What did that mean? I did not know, really, what that meant until the other kids made fun of me and called me "stupid." I felt stupid. I told my mom I was stupid. My pride was hurt because I didn't feel like the other kids, or I didn't feel like I belonged. Everyone seemed to have fun and school stuff was easy for them. . . .
>
> I had one friend like me, and we started a club only for kids like me. My teacher told my parents that I might have a learning disease, and should have some tests. I had a tutor

---

in class discussions, but when I think of something to contribute, I just get blank looks. What makes perfect sense to me doesn't make sense logically to others. My professors think I add a lot of spice to discussions, but most of the kids never get the point I'm trying to make.

---

every day after school, and I learned the stuff real good at night, but at school I could not remember what I'd learned or the right way to do problems. . . .

In fifth grade I still had trouble learning, and people, especially my teachers, were getting more and more mad at me for forgetting. Sometimes, I would forget all the stuff and have fun. Sometimes I would not. Mostly, not.

My mom really tried really, really hard to help me remember things, and she was starting to get mad at me, too. They told me I was not trying. The teacher told my mom I was lying about not remembering and that I was lazy. I'm not lazy. I'm just so tired of people telling me to try harder. I did not blame them for my disease, so why does everybody blame me?

He goes on and describes a terrible thing that happened at school, when he was forced by a teacher to pick up trash because he wouldn't do his homework. Kids started calling him the "Trash Man" and the name stuck.

I wish I could say that this is the only letter like this we have received at Focus on the Family. Unfortunately, it is not. These young people, without proper parental and medical care, can easily become defeated, first academically, then emotionally, then socially, and even spiritually. Yet, with proper care, these specially gifted kids can have academic success—they can discover who God has created them to be and find what He has in store for them.

The same thing happens when I'm looking at mathematical problems. I remember one day when I was looking through a book of brainteasers with my friends. We came to a problem that we all wanted to do. Within 25 seconds, I had figured out the answer to the problem. My friends were at it for another 10 minutes. The time difference was not what impressed everyone . . . it was the method I had used to solve the problem. No one understood what I had done, even though I tried to explain it. My approach was not even in the answer section of the book. I'm not saying that I'm brilliant, but I do think I'm blessed with thinking in a unique way because of being ADHD. I know that my mind goes much faster than others, and I can see ways to solve problems that they can't.

I even look at engineering problems differently from my fellow students. I can usually figure out unusual solutions to projects, but I couldn't tell you how I got there!

Coaches and professors associate learning disabilities with being unintelligent, rather than as a different way of learning. Because I've been diagnosed with this disability, I'm entitled to have 30 percent longer to take an exam, but I've always been reluctant to ask for that time because I don't know how a professor will react. Most professors automatically look down on you if they know you have ADHD. There is a professor in the education department at Dartmouth who has even said publicly that any kid with a learning disability doesn't belong in an Ivy League institution.

Even though I am entitled legally to have extra time on assignments, I never ask for it for fear the professor will think I'm trying to get out of something. I took an engineering quiz the other day, and I knew the answers to every question. But I was able to finish only half of it. I would have a better GPA if I took advantage of the legislation, but I just don't want to deal with the embarrassment and the hassle.

Although I have some distractive and hyperactive tendencies in my ADHD testing results, my real problem happens in lecture classes. I can hang on to the first couple of words uttered by a professor, but then there seems to be a roadblock. By the time my brain has sorted out the sentence, I have missed the rest of the information. Lectures with the professor as a talking head are pretty useless, but if he uses overheads, or if the class notes are on the Web, I'll do great with processing the data.

My learning disability resulted in really bad communication with my college softball coach. Most coaches rely on oral instructions to relay their ideas and wisdom to their players; however, the oral part just doesn't work for me. I need to be shown the concept. My coaches lost confidence that I would be a star player at the collegiate level because I just couldn't understand their instructions. Game after game and practice after practice, my coaches would yell at me for "not listening" to what they had told me to do, and I couldn't make them understand that I *was* listening . . . perhaps more intently than anyone else on the team. I just couldn't get those words to make sense in my head.

Finally, in my junior year, after I had the testing done for ADHD, I figured out what was wrong. For example, my softball coach had explained to me time and time again what needed to be done when there's a runner on first base and a runner on third base. As the shortstop, there were three things that I might have to do. Every time a first and third situation would happen, I would frantically try to review what she had verbally told me, but every time I messed it up. One day she decided to draw it on the board. I went back out on the field, and I haven't messed up a first and third situation since then. I only wish she had used that teaching method from day one of my freshman season.

I missed a lot because I learned differently than my fellow players. Most coaches don't have the patience to work with the "odd" athlete. So many kids with ADHD are treated this way . . . like they're stupid. They are stuck in a world that doesn't understand them while they are doing everything in their power to make sense of their daily lives. It makes me wonder how many brilliant minds—musicians, athletes, writers, and so on—we've lost because no one was willing to teach them in a way that they were able to understand.

I can't say it has been easy for me in college. Dartmouth has a 10-week term, so the coursework is very fast-paced, and a lot of ground is covered in a short amount of time. I do have to work harder than my friends, and being in a Division I athletic program further complicates things. However, despite all the problems, I think I am having a more fulfilling college experience than many other kids because I have to intentionally work harder than they do. Just because I have a learning disability is no reason to put the brakes on what I can accomplish. People are always complimenting me because I'm involved in so many activities. I think I have a more exciting life than they do because of my energy and my interest in a lot of different things. I wouldn't trade the way I am for anything.

Lessons Learned

1. Children with learning differences are very teachable; they simply have a different way of processing information.
2. Children with learning differences can do very well in college. An ADHD diagnosis should not discourage kids or their parents about their potential to achieve success in school and career.
3. Because they process information "out of the box," individuals with ADHD have great creative potential.
4. IQ is unrelated to learning disorders.

Reflection

Diane: I've often wondered about the truth of the saying "Ignorance is bliss." Since I never acknowledged that Danielle had a disability when she was growing up, I didn't treat her any differently from our older daughter. She took a lot more physical energy to raise, but we never made a big deal out of her unique way of responding to the world. If we had realized that she had a learning disability early on, would it have made a difference for her in school? I now often wonder if we could have made things easier for her.

Dennis: Finally understanding why I had struggled all through childhood made a huge impact on me. I felt as if a block of concrete had been removed from my chest! There was a verifiable reason for my struggles that no longer made me feel weird or different. I think that Lauree and I are much more understanding parents because we realize why our ADHD son, Dusty, behaves the way he does. We are more encouraging and more patient than we would be if we just felt he was goofing off.

Questions for Parents

What is your attitude toward your child's disability? Do you ever sense that your child thinks that there is something horribly wrong with him because you approach his disability with fear . . . or maybe even anger? Is it time for you and the rest of the family to work together to understand the disability to the extent that you all can help make life a bit more manageable for this particular child? Is it time for reflection and reassessment?

Therefore encourage one another and build each other up, just as in fact you are doing. ... And we urge you, brothers, warn those who are idle, encourage the timid, help the weak, be patient with everyone. (1 Thessalonians 5:11, 14)

4

All about Dusty

Think of [an ADHD person as] an absentminded
professor who can find a cure for cancer
but not his glasses in the mess on his desk.
These are the inventors, creators, poets—the people
who think creative thoughts because they
don't think like everyone else.
—MARTHA DENCKLA, M.D.[1]

Dennis: An ADHD parent raising an ADHD child is enough to try anyone's sanity. However, there are a lot of us out there. Most of the professionals I've talked with in the last several years say that the tendency to have ADHD is inherited. According to Dr. Bill Maier, Psychologist in Residence at Focus on the Family, "ADHD tends to run in families. Approximately one-half of parents who had ADHD have a child with the disorder. Unfortunately, many of these parents have never been formally diagnosed or treated. This can contribute to marital problems, parent-child conflict, and in some cases, violence."

Lauree and I recognized in Dusty's preschool days that he was not interested in reading or being read to. He wanted hands-on types of experiences, like playing with his toy wrestlers. He enjoyed television and playacting, just like I did as a child. As a matter of fact, I saw a lot of myself in Dusty at this age.

We were both hard of hearing in the preschool years, and our vocabularies suffered as a result. Dusty had constant ear infections as a child, and his doctor told us that for the first two years of his life he was not able to hear properly. (Diane tells me that Danielle suffered from the same, and even had to be hospitalized for chronic ear infections.) Dusty and I were also similar in that we didn't catch everything that was said to us, and therefore, we "turned inward" and withdrew from others to a certain degree. We entertained ourselves. And, as you've already read, I turned toward entertaining others as I grew older to hide my learning deficits.

It was at this time, during the preschool years, that Lauree and I noticed that Dusty was not developing at the same

Is there a genetic link with ADHD?

Dr. Larimore: There is increasing evidence from medical studies that genetic factors play a role in ADHD. Jacquelyn Gillis and her team, then at the University of Colorado, reported in 1992 that the risk of ADHD in a child whose identical twin has the disorder is between 11 and 18 times greater than that of a non-twin sibling of a child with ADHD.[2] She showed that between 55 and 92 percent of the identical twins of children with ADHD eventually develop the condition.

A large study of twins in Norway, involving 526 identical twins (who inherit exactly the same genes) and 389 fraternal twins (who are no more alike genetically than siblings born years apart), found that ADHD had nearly an 80 percent chance of being inherited. They concluded that up to 80 percent of the differences in attention, hyperactivity, and impulsivity between people with ADHD and those without the disorder can be explained by genetic factors.[3]

rate as other kids his age. He seemed about two years behind them. We had already noticed the difference between him and his brother, Chad, but we didn't want to face it. We kept hoping that he would catch up. We finally made the decision to hold him back in kindergarten.

Lauree and I had Dusty tested when he was six years old by a psychologist. I broke down and cried that day when the doctor gave us an explanation of Dusty's disability because it was only then—when I was an *adult*—that I finally had some definition of my own experience, which was now being repeated with my son. I can't tell you what it meant to finally have an explanation for why I was the way I was and to have HOPE—for Dusty and for me—that we were really OK! We were just two people who learned a little differently from the rest of the world.

In hindsight, Lauree and I should have gotten Dusty one-

In addition, scientists are telling us that there are genetic mechanisms that regulate hyperactivity, especially as they relate to dopamine. For example, a significant percentage of people with ADHD have been found to have an abnormality of the dopamine D4 receptor gene, which is associated with abnormal risk-taking behavior and hyperactivity.

What does this mean for your family? Simply that one or both of the parents of your ADHD child are likely to have ADHD. If so, dealing with your child may remind you of some painful memories from your childhood or teenage years. This can make it even more difficult and emotional to deal with your child. Furthermore, the unaffected siblings may be more likely to have children of their own with ADHD. These are just a few of the reasons that many ADHD therapists will recommend that parents and siblings also be tested for ADHD and consider education and counseling for the entire family.

on-one help as soon as he entered school, or perhaps we should have gone the home-schooling route. What Dusty needed was a classroom situation with only a couple of other kids around. They say hindsight is always 20/20, but we just didn't recognize that most school situations are not equipped to deal with kids like Dusty, and many teachers don't have the time or training to meet the needs of these kids.

It's been such an uphill struggle to do what is right for Dusty over the years. We did get him tutoring help in the middle of elementary school, and it was a good decision.

My emotions during these early years with Dusty fluctuated between guilt, anger, and depression because I *knew* he had inherited his problems from me. I felt so responsible. I hurt so much for the kid because I knew exactly what he was experiencing in school and that the days ahead wouldn't be any better. It was so difficult to be optimistic. I had made it, but I constantly wondered if Dusty would have the determination to overcome the challenges that would come his way. I still find myself thinking, *How will this kid ever make a living? Am I going to have to stay with him his entire life?* I wonder if my own daddy thought the same thing about me when I was growing up: *Will Dennis ever amount to anything?*

You would think I would have a lot of patience with Dusty, but more often than not, I find myself losing it with him. Lauree is always having to intercede on his behalf, saying, "Take it easy, Honey. He didn't mean to do it!" In a lot of ways, she is more patient with Dusty than I am.

It's a struggle for Dusty to get decent grades, so we enrolled him in Sylvan Learning Centers to help him improve his learning skills. One day, I missed a golf game in order to get him to his tutoring lesson. I admit I was a little upset about having to make that sacrifice, so I started to lecture Dusty in the car.

"Is this Sylvan place helping you, Son? It costs money you know! I didn't have this kind of help when I was a kid.

You're one lucky dude to be getting this help, but your mommy and I are willing to make the sacrifice, even if it is costing us an arm and a leg, if it's really helping you, Boy!"

I waited a few seconds for Dusty to answer my question, but he was watching a guy on a motorcycle who was next to us at the stoplight. Dusty finally responded, "Daddy, do motorcycles have air conditioning on them?"

"THINK ABOUT IT, SON!" I yelled. I completely lost it. When we got to Sylvan, I left Dusty in the car and I went inside to calm down. I have to keep remembering how hard it was for me to process information when I was a kid and be understanding with Dusty.

Dusty gets so excited about things that he acts before he puts his mind in gear. Once he was in the passenger seat of our new Suburban when he begged Lauree to let him push the button that opens the gate on the driveway. Well, he got so anxious about pushing the button that he pushed it again before the car was all the way through the gate. As the gate closed, it scratched the whole side of that sparkling new car! I knew something was wrong when Lauree came out to meet me when I came home from work.

"I don't want you to get mad, Honey. Dusty didn't mean to do it! Tell him it's OK. His little heart is broken."

It took every ounce of restraint to keep from yelling what was really on my mind, but I went into Dusty's bedroom and sat down on the bed. "Don't worry about it, Son. I want you to get a good night's sleep. I know that you didn't mean to wreck the car."

The look on Dusty's face made my self-restraint worth it. He was so relieved. He expected to be blasted, but it would have been wrong for me to do that. After all, it could have been me doing the same thing at his age.

You see how important it is to remember their good qualities? ADHD kids have many positive traits, but it's up to us to be patient and draw those traits out. Sometimes it helps to recall that throughout the Bible the people God often chose to bless were the unlikely candidates, the underdogs. A number of Bible heroes seemed to have ADHD traits (see chapter nine); they were diamonds in the rough God chose in order to show His power and glory.

Like those biblical characters, ADHD kids are also jewels in the rough. Raising them is like polishing a diamond. It takes a lot of energy, but they can make the world fun. Many love to laugh and make others feel good. That helps to balance out the frustrations they bring, doesn't it? Life with Dusty in the house is a blessing, despite the stories I've just related. He lives out the biblical adage to "rejoice with those who rejoice; mourn with those who mourn" (Romans 12:15). He is the first to shed tears in our family when he can sense someone is hurt or disappointed.

In the 2001 football season, Dusty played nose guard and center on the high school team. His team lost a playoff game, and when I went down on the field afterward Dusty was crying—not for himself or his disappointment, but for the seniors on the team who had wanted so much to win a championship their last year in high school. It gave me great satisfaction to watch my son throughout the season displaying this tendency to encourage and to be sensitive to his fellow players. He was the first to put his arm around an injured player, the first to speak a positive word to a frustrated coach, the first to appreciate a sports fan's "Good game" with, "Thanks, we couldn't do it without you!"

What is ironic is that he maintains this attitude despite the fact that he is always in trouble with the coaches for forgetting his shoes, his football pants, his jersey. He has to do laps after practice—*all the time*! So I guess you could say that his ADHD works for him and against him *all the time*. However, the positives far outweigh the negatives.

Dusty's ADHD dividends show up every Sunday and Wednesday when it comes to attending church services. He loves church, and in our family he is the first up and the first dressed and the first to leave. His love for the Lord was never more evident than following a tragic car accident involving three of his friends. One was killed and two injured—one with serious brain damage. Dusty was at the hospital with his friends, praying, supporting, and encouraging . . . standing strong as a Christian witness.

These are the things that make me so proud of Dusty as a human being. They don't measure these types of characteristics on the SAT or ACT tests, but these are the "test results" that matter the most to me as his father—the caliber of his character.

A couple of years ago I took Dusty to a Super Bowl game. It was a major feat just to get the tickets. When we got there, I guess I shouldn't have been surprised that they were lousy seats. I really had a tough time enjoying the game because I was so upset about the seats. I turned to Dusty and commented on the situation, and he grinned back at me, "But Dad, these are great seats! We can see what the blimp sees!" All of a sudden, I had a new perspective about the situation, and it turned out to be a great Super Bowl.

You would think I would have shared Dusty's perspective early on, since we are alike in so many ways, but I had gotten so caught up in the fact that I had paid big bucks for lousy seats that I no longer viewed the situation through the eyes of a child.

After the game, I prayed, "Is he going to make it in this world, Lord?" And I got my answer, "Yes, because ADHD kids see the big picture. They see life through a wonderful set of lenses!" ADHD kids, like Dusty, can see what the blimp sees.

Lessons Learned

1. Parents who are ADHD often have children with ADHD.
2. ADHD kids often see the world through different eyes than other people. Their unique way of looking at the

world—their ability to see the big picture—is a refreshing characteristic that should be lauded by all those who are so focused in their observations that they miss the forest for the trees.

3. ADHD kids respond better to encouragement than to criticism. They have difficulty processing verbal commands, especially if they are given in anger.

4. Since ADHD children thrive on encouragement, they often have the capacity to be great encouragers themselves.

Reflection

Dennis: At the beginning of this chapter, Dr. Bill Maier wrote that ADHD is a characteristic that runs in families. I often think that one of the reasons I lose my patience with Dusty more often than Lauree does is because we are so alike. His foul-ups remind me of my foul-ups, and so my impatience contains a little bit of self-directed anger as well. And sometimes I am terribly defensive about Dusty for the same reason—I'm super sensitive to what he is going through.

Diane: I had a really huge problem dealing with a couple of Danielle's softball coaches over the years. When I was in the car following a game, I would often verbalize this frustration, which did no one any good. It was particularly hard on Danielle, who would internalize my mood. So I know how defensive one can be when you feel your kid isn't getting a fair shake. It feels like a time bomb inside your soul that simmers week after week until some incident or somebody's insensitive remark sets it off, leaving you feeling like a modern-day impersonation of Dr. Jekyll and Mr. Hyde. I think I have spent more time in prayer about this than any other single thing in my life.

Question for Parents
Do you find your child difficult to put up with because you're so similar?

> *More than that, we rejoice in our sufferings, knowing that suffering produces endurance, and endurance produces character, and character produces hope, and hope does not put us to shame, because God's love has been poured into our hearts through the Holy Spirit who has been given to us.* (Romans 5:3-5, ESV)

5

Will This Kid Ever Amount to Anything?

The same right-brained children who are being labeled and shamed in our schools are the very individuals who have the skills necessary to lead us into the 21st century. These children process visually and randomly, and think holistically. They are intuitive problem solvers who get the big picture. They thrive on visual imagery and stimulation; these "attention-deficit" kids can spend hours with computer and CD-ROM programs that mirror their thought processes. It's no wonder they are attracted to computers. The use of computers is congruent with the way right-brained children think.
—JEFFREY FREED and LAURIE PARSONS[1]

One concern that many parents of ADHD children share is the secret fear that their kids will end up living on the dole because they won't be able to hold down a job when they become young adults. *Will his employer think the same way about him as all of his teachers have over the years? Will I have to support this kid my entire life? He can't even get both of his shoes tied without losing attention, so how will he ever hold down a job?*

During some of our more exhausting moments in raising Danielle and Dusty we've had this thought: *Wouldn't it be great to be able to wave a magic wand and disengage this kid from all the behaviors that are driving me up the wall at this very moment?* Fortunately, neither of us was omnipotent, so our kids have survived intact.

Your child and ADHD are together like peanut butter and jelly. And the Lord created him or her that way—uniquely special. Jesus was always putting things together that didn't seem to work very well. He said that the meek would inherit the earth. He promised that those who were hungry would be filled. He said that He gave us a yoke that lifted us up. He healed us by being wounded. He told us that we live by dying and receive by giving. Is turning what our educational system considers a disorder into a dividend beyond His control? We don't think so!

There have been many gifted people over the years in all fields of endeavor who have turned their disabilities into dividends. Helen Keller was 19 months old when brain fever left her without sight and hearing. And yet this remarkable woman, with the intervention of a gifted teacher, Miss Anne Sullivan, was able to graduate from Radcliffe College with honors at the turn of the last century. She went on to champion the cause of the handicapped in speeches and in her writings. Her inspirational life story was made into a movie, and her victory over seemingly insurmountable odds continues to inspire students all over the world.

An article in *USA Today* contained the kind of story that makes wonderful copy for sportscasters everywhere. A very special young man was nominated to carry the Olympic torch in the relay leading to the 2002 Winter Games. Nick Ackerman was a college senior who won the 2001 NCAA Division III national title in wrestling despite having both legs amputated below the knees. He is quoted as saying, "I just read a poem one of my teachers gave me. One of the lines was something like, 'You are the handicap you must face. You're the one that chooses your place.'" After the final match in the National Championships, a reporter was said to have asked Nick about being disabled. He responded, "Don't call me disabled." When asked what he would prefer, he responded, "Call me a national champ if you want."[2]

What a lesson for anybody diagnosed with a learning "disability"! Perhaps it should only be considered a disability if you consider it to be one. Think about other remarkable people with handicaps who accomplished great things: Beethoven was deaf when he wrote some of his most remarkable music. Van Gogh was in a mental hospital when he painted some of his most beautiful paintings. And then there is the magical name of Walt Disney.

We were kids when Disneyland was constructed in Anaheim, California. We can still remember the excitement that the theme park generated all over the world when it opened. Fantasy had become reality! We can still feel the excitement in the pit of our stomachs over the very special vacation days spent there. What type of mind would envision such a place? And further, what type of person could take that vision and make it a reality? We think Walt Disney displayed many of the characteristics of a person with ADHD, and that this unique way of looking at the world was what gave us Walt Disney cartoons and eventually the Disneyland theme parks.

One morning in 1948, Disney elected not to go to his studio at all but play hooky instead. He donned his striped engineer's uniform and his railroad hat, and slipped behind the controls of his beloved "Carol Pacific," a miniature train he had built on tracks that circled the perimeter of his home. As he rode his train, he tried to piece together in his mind an idea that he had toyed with for the past 13 years—since visiting the Statue of Liberty. He had circled the house a good half-dozen times when his train suddenly jumped the track and slammed into the side of a 90-foot S-shaped tunnel he had installed. It didn't stop there. It crashed through the living room wall before coming to a halt—something that must have really made his wife's day since she had recently purchased new furniture! Out of this type of mind—one that

---

Is ADHD associated with risk-taking behaviors like tobacco abuse, alcoholism, drug abuse, or crime?

Dr. Larimore: Some studies indicate that there is an association between ADHD and the abuse of alcohol and drugs, as well as criminal activity. When it comes to tobacco abuse, a study from the University of California, Berkeley,[3] reported "a significant difference in rates of daily smoking and tobacco dependence for those with ADHD who had used stimulant medication in childhood in contrast to controls." These researchers felt there was a possible link between ADHD treatment histories and levels of tobacco dependence in adulthood.

However, most experts believe these antisocial behaviors are much more likely in those who have ADHD and another disorder, such as conduct disorders and mental health disorders. They believe those who have ADHD alone, and who are treated with medication, do not appear to be at increased risk for these problems. In fact, they point to a study that showed that medication for children with ADHD reduced the probability of substance use disorder (SUD) by 85 percent when compared with the risk among unmedicated kids with ADHD.[4]

The general danger of the typical characteristics of ADHD, particularly in adolescence and adulthood, is a desire for high-risk activity. Dr. Dobson points out, "Even as children, they can be accident-prone. But, as they get older, rock climbing, bungee jumping, car racing, motor-

could be so distracted as to wreak havoc on his home—came the vision for the theme parks we all love today.[5]

Similarly, children and adults with ADHD characteristics exhibit impulsive behavior. Unfortunately, this usually doesn't end in multimillion dollar ideas like Walt Disney's did. These people are often inattentive and easily bored. For example, Diane never was able to take Danielle on a shopping trip that lasted longer than 45 minutes, even if the purpose of the trip was to purchase something Danielle really

---

cycle riding, white-water rafting and other high-risk activities are among their favorite activities."[6]

Thus, "Adults with ADHD are sometimes called 'adrenaline junkies,' because they are hooked on the 'high' produced by the adrenaline rush associated with dangerous behavior. Others are more susceptible to drug use, alcoholism, and other addictive behaviors."[7] Consequently, about 40 percent of adolescents living with ADHD have been arrested by their eighteenth birthday.[8]

Dr. Dobson warns those with ADHD: "Some adults who have ADHD are at higher risk for marital conflict, too. It can be very irritating to a compulsive, highly ordered husband or wife to be married to a 'messie'—someone whose life is chaotic and one who forgets to pay the bills, fix the car, or keep records for income-tax reports. Such a couple usually need professional counseling to help them learn to work together and capitalize on each other's strengths."[9]

Nevertheless, for many who live with ADHD, the symptoms will diminish with neurologic social maturing. Nevertheless, it is helpful for all of us to realize that many of those living with ADHD can, with instruction, skill, and mentoring, demonstrate in remarkable ways their outstanding giftedness—which can include creativity, energy, enterprising thinking, and leadership skills.

wanted. She would become unbelievably restless and bored with the entire experience. (Some man will be grateful for this characteristic some day. Imagine a woman who hates to shop!) Even when Danielle became a young adult, Diane intentionally planned their shopping excursions like an army general planning Operation Desert Storm: There were clearly defined objectives to the trips that could be accomplished in one or two stores within half an hour. Anything longer and it was, "MOOOOOMMM! This is so boring! Can't we do something else? I really don't need another pair of jeans. My old ones are fine. Let's get outta here!"

Diane cannot remember one time, prior to leaving for college, when Danielle actually packed her own belongings for a camping or athletic trip or vacation. Her attention span was fine for the first several items that went into her bag—the first of which was usually a ball or a game. But her sister, Nicole, often had to make sure Danielle had everything she needed in her suitcase before leaving. It always seemed an impossibility for Danielle to gather her thoughts and her attention to take care of this 30-minute chore unless Mom or Sis was in the room looking over her shoulder and keeping her focused.

ADHD children tend to be restless, and as a result, are noncompliant in situations that require compliance. For example, getting an ADHD kid ready for school can start the entire day off on the wrong foot for a parent. These kids forget their jackets, their lunch boxes, and their homework. Dennis recalls one day in particular when he yelled three times at Dusty because he was going to miss the school bus if he didn't hurry and finish his breakfast: " 'HURRY UP!' I hollered. He gave me this blank look from the dining table and responded, 'Daddy, could a bazooka come through that wall right there?'"

These characteristics can drive a parent nuts! Dennis recalls another incident:

It was January, really cold, and my turn to drive my sons to the Christian school, which was about 20 miles from our home. We were almost at school when Dusty started to cry in the backseat.

"Daddy, you're going to be mad at me . . . really mad."

"What is it, Son?"

"You're going to really be mad, Dad!"

I gripped the steering wheel and ground my teeth, "I won't be mad. What is it?"

"I forgot my shoes!"

I lost it! "Couldn't you figure that out walking from the house to the car?"

Dusty's big brother started in making excuses for him, which just made me madder! "He didn't mean to forget the shoes, Dad. Give him a break. We all make mistakes!"

But I ignored Chad because I was so mad, and I just screamed louder. "You're going to school just the way you are! I'm *not* going back for those shoes! And Chad, since you're making so many excuses for your brother, you can go to the office with him because I'm not leaving this car!"

Later I called Lauree and told her what happened. I screamed into the phone, "HE'S GOT TO LEARN RESPONSIBILITY! IF YOU WANT HIM TO HAVE SHOES, YOU'LL HAVE TO BRING THEM BECAUSE I'M NOT GOING TO!" Lauree responded in her sweetest voice that I had every right to be mad, but that I was wrong to make Chad assume the parent role by taking Dusty to the office. She had a point there, and in hindsight, I should have handled the situation differently and gone into the office with Dusty. But this kind of thing happens all the time with kids who have ADHD, and parents do lose it once in a while.

However, the same ADHD adults or children who can drive teachers, employers, parents, and spouses nuts with certain characteristics also have traits that are so admirable, so valuable, that if reinforced make them people to be reckoned with. It is as if their brain chemistry enables them to size up people and situations much more quickly than the average person. They have intuitive capabilities that lead to creative problem solving, and when this is paired with their high

---

Dr. Larimore: I'll never forget meeting Sarah. She was failing her college classes. She had gone through four roommates, each complaining of her messiness and lack of organization. She was a social butterfly known for her creativity and energy. Yet her study habits were atrocious. She felt she had made it through high school based upon her ability to talk her way through difficult academic situations.

Sarah had recently been arrested for a DUI and marijuana was found in the car. Her favorite memories included bungee jumping and skydiving. But she was seeing me for depression. She had trouble sleeping and had "no friends left."

Although I sensed she was depressed and that her self-esteem was at rock bottom, I wondered if there wasn't something else going on. Her lab tests were all normal. Her depression-screening questionnaire was borderline positive. But her Conner's Scale questionnaire for ADHD was very high.

I told her, "Sarah, in a sense, even the word 'disorder' in ADHD is somewhat misleading, because the syndrome has so many positive features." She wrinkled up her forehead and blurted out, "No way!"

"Way!" I responded. We laughed. Then, I pulled out a copy of an article from *Time* magazine and read this to her: "[People with ADHD] see themselves as creative; their impulsiveness can be viewed as spontaneity; hyperactivity gives them enormous energy and drive; even their distractibility has the virtue of making them alert to changes in the environment. People with ADHD are wild, funny, and effervescent. They have lots of life."[10]

energy levels, it is no wonder that so many of them become entrepreneurs, engineers, artists, and problem solvers.

In Danielle's first engineering class at Dartmouth, the professor challenged the students to develop and test a project that had not been attempted before. Since she loves to

---

"Sounds like me!" she exclaimed.

"I agree. Furthermore, Sarah, ADHD can almost always be treated successfully with a number of therapies. Wanna learn more?"

"You bet!"

The more I discussed ADHD with Sarah, the more her eyes lit up. I asked Sarah to see a psychiatrist experienced in caring for adults and adolescents with ADHD to confirm the diagnosis and to rule out any other possible causes for her symptoms. She agreed.

The psychiatrist spent a fair amount of time with Sarah and her parents. By the end of the consultation, all agreed ADHD was the likely diagnosis. They discussed treatment options and together agreed to begin family therapy. Sarah also chose to try one of the longer-acting stimulant medications.

When I saw Sarah in my office just two weeks later, she was already doing, as she said, "One thousand percent better! The medication has helped me in so many ways. But the family counseling has just been great. Mom and Dad see me differently now. They're beginning to understand who I am and how I've been made. That makes me feel so much better 'cause they're beginning to love me just the way that I am—not the Sarah they wanted me to be. Not only that, we all think my brother may also be ADHD. And, although he hasn't yet admitted it, I think Daddy has it. So, we've got a long way to go, but Doc, you've got us heading down the right road."

Eventually, Sarah graduated with honors. Today she is in her last year of medical school and, no surprise to me, has chosen to specialize in psychiatry.

snowboard, Danielle decided to invent a lock that was built into the board so that keeping track of a key was not necessary. Burton Snowboards, a leader in the industry, gave her project team several boards on which to try out this invention. It was so successful that several companies have since expressed an interest in the patent. The professor laughingly commented to Danielle that hers was one of the most unusual ideas ever proposed in this particular course, and her team was given publicity in the alumni newsletter, a further singular occurrence.

During a break at a Focus on the Family Heritage Builders Conference in Colorado Springs, Dennis engaged in a conversation with a gentleman who owned a very successful, nationwide chain of restaurants. They shared their common experiences of growing up with ADHD. What impressed Dennis so much, however, was the vision and entrepreneurial spirit of this man. He had been incredibly successful as an adult, but was full of creative ideas for projects that he still wanted to accomplish.

Charles Schwab, the gentleman who almost single-handedly founded the discount brokerage business, has a learning disability that impacted him while growing up, and as a result is very sensitive to the pain that children endure when they are different from everyone else in the classroom. His advice to children who suffer with disabilities like he did is this: "You've just got to learn your way through it because there are some things you can do that others cannot, and there are some things others can do you're just not going to be able to do, ever. Now my experience has been that what works is to go a little bit slower. . . ."[12]

Although Schwab's disability was diagnosed as dyslexia, his brain works similarly to many children and adults who have ADHD. Diane's daughter Danielle has a similar way of problem solving as that admitted to by Schwab during an interview for *Fortune* magazine. He stated, "Many times I can see a solution to something and synthesize things differently and quicker than other people. . . . [In meetings], I would see the end zone and say, 'This is where we need to go.'" He continued by saying that his was an annoyance to sequential thinkers because it "shortcuts their rigorous step-by-step process."[13]

The important point to make to your child is that a diagnosis of ADHD is not a "death sentence." They are in the same boat as many successful folks who have overcome the differences of ADHD. One particularly interesting Internet site lists famous folks in several fields, including the arts, business, science, sports, and entertainment, that you may wish to explore with your child. If for no other purpose, it will give a healthy dose of self-esteem to the child who may be struggling with some of the same issues that these folks did! So check out SchwabLearning.org with your child.

Lessons Learned

1. Learning differences can be overcome and may even become assets.
2. Successful people who have been diagnosed as adults with ADHD have used their unique ways of looking at the world to their benefit—they have changed a disability into an asset.
3. Parents are essential in helping children understand that ADHD is not a bad thing; it's a different thing!

Reflection

Dennis: I know that a measurement for progress is important in school, so we can't really do away with grades. I only wish that kids with ADHD could see beyond the structure of their world as defined by their school surroundings. The famous people I've read about who have or may have had ADHD have survived in spite of school. This is a sad commentary. The kid who looks out the window at school and daydreams can become the adult with the drive and ambition to make it big. However, they will never know that if they only pay attention to their ranking in class or their latest test scores or the teacher's often harsh reprimands.

I've read the life stories of several prominent people in the last several years: singer Harry Belafonte, mystery writer Dame Agatha Christie, billionaire businessman Mal-

---

Dr. Larimore: Dr. Dobson writes, "Some adults with ADHD learn to be less disorganized and impulsive as they get older. They channel their energy into sports activities or professions in which they function very well."[11]

Studies have demonstrated that about 50 percent of adults with ADHD function normally, but the other half continue to have a wide variety of social difficulties. A small percentage have severe problems with their ADHD as adults. Nevertheless, with understanding parents, teachers, and career counselors, ADHD teens and young adults can find professions in which their attention deficit differences are a benefit.

A principle that I have found useful in helping them find their role in God's plan for their lives is teaching them to avoid the "you should" comments. Often, kids will hear teachers, coaches, Scout leaders, parents, or even a pastor tell them what they "should do." Now, when it comes to biblical absolutes, the "shoulds" are vital to being highly healthy. But when it comes to career choices, they may be harmful.

For example, Daryl was a patient of mine for over 15 years. His parents never quite understood this principle. Daryl did exceptionally well with his ADHD, but in college he took the courses his parents told him he should take, so that he could go into the career they thought he should pursue. When I saw him in the office, it was because he was flunking his course work. His parents thought I should change his treatment.

colm Forbes, and General George Patton. All of these people showed the capacity for accomplishment despite their inauspicious beginnings in school. I think children with ADHD need to be reminded constantly that what God will accomplish in their lifetimes, if they are submitted to Him, goes far beyond the classroom during their first 18 years on this planet.

As Daryl and I talked about his gifts and talents, as we explored those things that really gave him satisfaction and energy and interest, they all revolved around the entertainment world. It became clear to me that Daryl's parents were trying to create a marigold out of a daisy. But, as we talked, I focused Daryl's "shoulds" into "coulds" and "woulds." What he really wanted to do was to get into TV or theatre production. "I love that world, Dr. Walt," he told me, "but, my parents don't. They tell me I should do something else."

I encouraged Daryl's mom to allow Daryl to try an entertainment curriculum at his college. She reluctantly agreed. "I guess he couldn't do any worse!" she scoffed.

Daryl returned to school and I didn't see or hear from him for another year. We met at a Christmas party the next year. When he saw me, he just about ran across the room. "Dr. Walt, I've been wanting to see you," he exclaimed as he gave me a big bear hug. As he caught me up on the previous year I could sense his infectious enthusiasm. He loved the curriculum and was making all A's and B's. "I'm going into the television production business," he told me with obvious self-satisfaction. "I'll be doing an internship at a local TV station this summer. Doc, I've really found myself."

Now, finding your place in life is difficult for many people without ADHD, but it's particularly difficult and important for those with ADHD to do this. We, as their friends, parents, teachers, pastors, youth leaders, and coaches, must be part of this process. Let's not lay our "shoulds" on their "coulds" and "woulds."

Diane: When I was in my early teens, my mother used to say to me, "The best friends you will make in life come after you graduate from high school." Although I didn't say so to her face, I didn't believe her at the time. I thought, *What could matter more than high school? I'll always remember EVERYTHING about this time, and I'll always be best friends with so and so.*

Well, I'm on the other side of age 50 now, and the last time I set eyes on one of my high school acquaintances was about four years ago. The friends I have now didn't even grow up in the same state that I did. All this to say that it would be so much easier on our ADHD kids if we could free their minds from the difficulties they are currently experiencing and open their eyes to the possibilities that lie ahead for them. One of my friends sent her severely ADHD child to Landmark College in Vermont, a campus specifically geared for young adults with learning disabilities. She told me, with a great deal of emotion, how her daughter's life had changed when she could actually see the possibilities available for her future. Our kids need to know that we serve a God of hope—One who has our future in the palm of His hand.

Questions for Parents

What does your child do best? Have you capitalized on this? Does he define himself by his school successes or by what he does better than anything else?

> *There are different kinds of gifts, but the same Spirit. There are different kinds of service, but the same Lord. There are different kinds of working, but the same God works all of them in all men.*
> (1 Corinthians 12:4-6)

6

The Battle Plan

Call upon me in the day of trouble;
I will deliver you, and you will honor me.
—PSALM 50:15

The Swanbergs and the Passnos are good examples of what most parents do when they learn they have a kid who has a learning disability. Denial is the name of the game! You have already read about the mental gymnastics that we both went through when it appeared Danielle and Dusty had problems. It's hard enough to admit it to yourself, much less to friends, who might not understand the disorder at all. According to a March 2000 Roper poll, almost two-thirds of Americans still associate learning disabilities with mental retardation.[1]

Some parents react to the diagnosis with a frenzy of activity. They go on the Internet and to the local bookstore and read everything they can put their hands on about the disorder. They run from article, to doctor, to school counselor, to another book, and finally, to a seminar to find a "cure" for little Johnny. The assumption is that Johnny will be a failure unless they step in immediately with the right intervention.

First of all, Johnny will not be a failure unless that is the

Learn as much about ADHD as you can

Dr. Larimore: Successful management of ADHD involves a range of options. However, the first and foremost, after diagnosis, is education. The person living with ADHD is usually greatly relieved to learn that he or she has an identifiable, treatable condition. They are gratified (as are their parents) to learn that they've done nothing wrong. This condition is not caused; you are born with it. It's part of your design and makeup. Best of all, God can and does use ADHD in His particular and peculiar plan for your life.

One organization that may be able to help is known as CHADD, which has an incredible amount of evidence-based and trustworthy information available and can offer the seeds, at least, for some parent support groups. This organization, and others, can help you gather information. However, let me share a caution here. Parent support groups, if not carefully done, can turn into gripe and whine sessions. That is not helpful and is sometimes harmful. All of us need someone to gripe to on occasion, no doubt, but unless there's some direction to the group, such as, "Okay, now that we've heard everyone's complaints, what can we do about it?" it just stays at the complaining level. Then the kids pay the price. I've known parents to come home from such a group and get all over their child because of what they talked about at the support group. That's not helpful for the parent or the child.

Also, you can contact Focus on the Family and find out how you can get a copy of the book *You and Your Child* (HarperCollins Australia, 1999). This paperback explains everything about ADHD, from the root causes of the disorder to treatment and other practical ways to deal with it, including how to teach an ADHD child in church. There is also a complimentary booklet we can send by Dr. James Dobson, *ADHD: Facts and Encouragement*. (Call 1-800-AFAMILY or log on to www.family.org to order these resources.)

Wherever you obtain information, be sure to look with a careful eye. Ask yourself: "Is this going to fit my child? Is this going to work in our family?"

expectation foisted on him by his frenzied parents and frustrated teacher. As we have attempted to show in the preceding chapter, ADHD can be an incredible dividend, and there are countless success stories to attest to that. The key is finding the right physician, the right educational program, and the right structure at home for your child. (We will cover the school situation in the next chapter.)

So where is a parent to begin? We intentionally chose the Bible verse from Psalm 50 to open this chapter because the first step is to stop and pray. The Lord made your child. Your child is infinitely more precious to Him than to even you!

Often, prayers for our children can be filled with a great deal of pain because we identify so strongly with their emotions and struggles. Diane can remember feeling Danielle's frustration in relating to her college softball coach. It bothered Diane so much that she often found herself asking God's forgiveness for the anger she felt on behalf of Danielle. That anger, that sense of injustice, was felt so strongly that it was often difficult to pray. She finally resorted to writing out her prayers because it was the only way to get her thoughts together enough to ask for the Lord's intervention and direction for Danielle.

Danielle called home, her voice trembling with emotion, one particular day. "It's so hard to go on sometimes, Mom. My coach associates my learning disability and energy level with being out of control. I don't know if I can ever make her think any differently about me. She's wrong, but I will never get the chance to prove it."

When a parent's soul is so deeply intertwined with their child's emotions, praying for direction is often the hardest thing in the world to sit down and do. Diane often didn't even know how to pray for Danielle in this particular situation. Nevertheless, daily, during the three years Danielle played college softball, she prayed fervently for the Lord's divine intervention. He answered, but not in the way she anticipated or hoped. Danielle called one day and announced that she felt the Lord was telling her to give up college athletics and the sport she loved to spend more time with other activities like the Navigators group on campus.

Only God knows the paths our children will take in life. Our expectations of how things will go for them—the careers they will eventually have, where they will live, and whom they will marry—rarely turn out the way we plan. Despite the uncertainties that lie ahead for our kids, God is the anchor we must cling to, and prayer is the means by which we receive not only direction, but assurance for the decisions we make for their education and medical treatment. So take your child's problem to God and seek His guidance. And then, wait upon the Lord for discernment and direction. He is so faithful to provide answers when we don't know which way to turn. Different parents will choose different solutions for their children's treatment as a result of this. The Lord did not make "cookie cutter" children, and so we should not expect "cookie cutter" answers from Him for kids with ADHD.

If you've ever picked up *Consumer Reports*, you have found a rating for just about every gadget you could ever want to buy. Unfortunately, we have better information about electric shavers and clothes dryers than we do about the abilities of our hometown physicians who treat ADHD. There are resources available to you in searching for just the right doctor for your child, but we would recommend that you talk to parents with ADHD kids first. It's amazing what information is available by simply asking friends for their help. Of course, the local city or county medical association can give referrals, as can your family doctor, and there is also information on the Internet from national ADHD organizations. Remember: Not every kind, loving, general practitioner is ready to take on the "blessings" of treating your ADHD child! You need to find someone with experience in treating the condition—someone who can communicate well with your child.

Once you have selected a physician, we recommend that you see him first without your child present. Ask him about his experience in treating children with ADHD. Ask him about his philosophy in treating these children. Does he or she seem to be the type of doctor who can talk simply and clearly with a child? Do you understand what he is saying to you? Don't be afraid to ask the hard questions that have been

---

Get the most accurate diagnosis possible

Dr. Larimore: Admittedly, a lot of things that look like ADHD may not be. What are you to do? You can clearly see your child is having difficulty. How can you find out what's really going on?

First of all, it is unwise for you to attempt to make the diagnosis yourself—or even to allow a teacher to do so. The guidelines in this chapter can be helpful, but this is not a diagnosis to try to make without professional help. There are many other problems, both psychological and physical, that can cause similar symptoms. Thyroid disorders, for example, can make a child hyperactive or sluggish; depression or anxiety can cause a form of distractibility that can be identical to that seen with ADHD. Obviously, this calls for professional help.

Consult a family physician, pediatrician, child developmentalist, doctor of psychology, or psychiatrist who specializes in ADHD, and who can effectively evaluate the problems. You want someone who is aware of the limitations of diagnosing ADHD, who knows what the criteria are for defining the syndrome, and who can do the appropriate psychological and neurological testing. And the sooner you can get that youngster in to see the specialist, the better.

Now, how do you find this expert? In most larger communities, there will inevitably be at least one or two pediatricians and family physicians who have a particular interest and involvement in managing behavioral issues. By far the best experts to ask for recommendations are parents who have one of these kids.

nagging you, even if you feel embarrassed. It is important that you leave this first appointment feeling comfortable. You want your child to get the best treatment possible, so get all of your questions answered. If you feel uncomfortable in the presence of the physician, your child will certainly pick up your "vibes" when it comes time for his or her first visit.

We also recommend that you prepare your child in advance for the visit with the physician. Be careful how you describe the technical term Attention Deficit Hyperactivity Disorder. That is a mouthful for any elementary-age child! Remember, your goal is not to win the drama critic's award for "Days of Our Lives." You need to be warm, natural, and encouraging in this dialogue. Empathize with little Johnny or Jenny. Your conversation could go something like this: "I know how hard it is to listen to dull teachers and to read hard books. I went through the same thing when I was your age. It was hard for me to sit still too. I know that it bothers you that you forget what you just heard, or that you can't follow instructions. Some instructions are so complicated that Einstein wouldn't get them! You're not dumb or lazy or stupid. You just learn things a little differently. This doctor is going to try to help you concentrate so school isn't so hard. I'll be right there with you."

Don't surprise your child with a visit to the doctor, or pressure or embarrass him ahead of time to force him to go. He needs enough time to adjust to the idea of going so that he can ask you questions and you can put him at ease. Most kids associate doctors with shots, crying, medicine, and all sorts of things they would like to avoid. So treat his uneasiness with care and consideration and explain exactly what will happen in the visit.

As parents, you will need to be prepared for the physician to talk to you about medication as one way of treating ADHD. Some folks are dead set against using prescription drugs to treat learning disorders; nevertheless, this will likely enter into the conversation sooner rather than later. Your child may have a problem with this as well because he has learned at school to "just say no" to drugs. If you and your doctor decide that medication is a course of action to take, you will need to help your child understand the difference between bad drugs that harm him and good drugs that help him.

One brief word about the medication issue (which will be discussed further by Dr. Larimore in subsequent chapters). Dr. Bill Maier, Psychologist in Residence at Focus on the Family, has words of caution for parents who have received misinformation about the use of medication leading to drug abuse later on for their youngsters: "The belief that treating ADHD children with stimulant medication will lead to later drug abuse is absolutely, unequivocally false. It is based on rumor, gossip, and the deliberate spreading of misinformation. In fact, children who truly have the disorder and are not properly treated have a higher likelihood of abusing drugs and alcohol as teenagers and young adults."

Part of your "battle plan," after you have selected the right physician, is something that needs to be a constant in the home: ADHD kids need an inordinate amount of encouragement, encouragement, and more encouragement! Dennis maintains that for every one negative word, an ADHD individual needs about seven positive words of reinforcement. This may be a bit of an exaggeration, but no one can deny the potency of the spoken word. Words are powerful. We can shape a child's life with them. Curt, painful remarks cut deep and can find a resting place in a young life for years.

Dennis has already related how a teacher's hurtful words were a turning point for him in the third grade. Likewise, words that a parent speaks in exasperation to a child with ADHD who has frustrated them beyond the point of endurance can cause emotional scarring. And ADHD children often become experts at masking the hurt. These kids need to know without any doubt that their parents believe in

Commit to giving your child unconditional love

Dr. Larimore: The most important treatment for children with ADHD is first to prescribe a lot of love. They very frequently are accused of not trying, of being lazy, of not being a good kid. Teachers get mad at them. Some classmates get upset with them because they don't do well in school, and they begin to treat them disrespectfully. My heart goes out to these youngsters.

Many times these kids feel like they are second-class. I've had kids in my practice tell me, "There's something wrong with me." I've had kids actually say, "God made a mistake when He put me together. That's why I'm here."

Part of loving ADHD kids is to help them discover the great giftedness that God has given them—to show them that God didn't make a mistake when He made them.

Children simply do not all have to fit the same mold, even in school. For many of these youngsters, parents may need to de-emphasize academics. Simply put, for many ADHD kids, there are things that are more important than academics, such as being loved and accepted by family and friends just the way that God made them. Your child needs to understand that God has a place for her and has given her a special gift, and that she does have specialized ability. She needs to know that you are going to work with her to discover and develop those special gifts and skills, and that you can't wait to see what God's going to do with her. This may be far more important to your ADHD child than getting too excited over the fact that she is not doing quite as well in the classroom as others.

Loving these kids unconditionally does not mean expecting them to do less than their best—the best that *they* can do. It does mean helping them discover their giftedness, recognizing their weaknesses, and directing and encouraging them to overcome challenges and achieve those things that they are gifted to do.

them. We constantly tell Dusty and Danielle how much we love them and how special they are, because they need that verbal fuel as they tackle the educational minefield that greets them each day.

"Dusty was really struggling with Spanish last semester, so he decided not to take it this term. Why? He flunked it! Yep, a BIG F!" recalls Dennis.

"Well, in order to receive a state scholarship for any school in Louisiana, a student has to have a B average and take Spanish. Spanish is not required to get into college, but it is if you want to qualify for the state-sponsored scholarship. When Dusty got the failing grade, he was so tense. He felt like a failure. Well, I told Dusty not to worry about a college scholarship, that I would see to it that he would get a college education. I told him to just concentrate on the basics—on math and English—because I loved him and believed in him. I know that he worked harder and longer than any of his friends, even though his grade was an F. He needed to hear from me that I thought of him as a success because of his effort and dedication to hard work."

It is our observation that many ADHD kids are enormous encouragers themselves if they have been the recipient of that kind of unconditional love. We have noticed this type of child readily understands the mind-set of the underdog because they've been there! They know what it is like to believe that they are "odd man out" in a classroom setting. A couple of years ago, Diane was complaining (again!) to Danielle about her college softball coach not giving her the chance to show what she could contribute to the season. Danielle listened to this verbal assault for a while, and then quietly said, "Mom, maybe God's place for me on this team was never the infield, but the bench. I know I've been an encouragement to team members who don't get to play very much. Maybe this is the role that the Lord has for me in college, rather than the starter role I had in high school." Diane was stunned into silence, for out of the mouth of her daughter had come a wonderful, godly response. Later, when Danielle told her coach that she would not compete her senior year of college softball, the coach responded, "I hope you reconsider because you are the soul of the team."

Danielle had lived out the word "encourager" by the way she had lived her life, even when profoundly discouraged about not playing more often. She had ministered to her teammates. Dusty too has been an encourager to others, particularly a younger boy in the neighborhood who has some physical problems to contend with. It brings tears to the eyes of parents when they witness this type of behavior being exhibited by a child who is supposed to be the "one with the problem." Now, that's not to say that every child with ADHD is naturally encouraging, but it's a trait we've often observed.

We also have another observation, which probably doesn't have any scientific data whatsoever to back it up, but ADHD children seem to be intensely spiritual. This is another reason we selected Psalm 50 to begin this chapter. If these kids have been introduced to Jesus Christ, they call out to Him loud and often! And at an early age. They seem to be more aware of their vulnerability than the average kid.

Dennis recalls with a mixture of embarrassment and pride Dusty's pronouncement that he had become a Christian: "I didn't believe it at first because he has such an imagination! One day Dusty announced to the family that he had accepted Jesus as his Savior. He was seven years old. Even his brother, Chad, said, 'You didn't get saved. You just want attention from Mom and Dad.' Well, I sat down with him on his bed and said, 'Are you sure you're not saying this or doing this just because of your folks and your brother?' Dusty said, 'I asked Jesus into my heart. I was jumping up and down on the trampoline by myself, and I got on my knees and asked Jesus into my heart.' So I said to him, 'Well let me lead you in prayer about that.' But Dusty replied, 'Why, Dad? I already did it!'

"Well, I'm not exactly proud of the fact that I still had trouble believing him, so I suggested we go out to the trampoline and that he show me what he'd done. After that, we went back to his bedroom, and I prayed a prayer of thanksgiving to the Lord for giving me such a special little boy. I went and got the camera and took a photo of Dusty so he would always remember that October 1st was his spiritual birthday."

Danielle and Dusty have wonderful consciences—they want to make right the things that they do wrong. Again, this seems to us to be a characteristic they share with many other kids with ADHD. They are often the first in the family to go to church because of their heart for God. Dusty plays that role in his family even though Dennis is a former pastor. Danielle attends church at Dartmouth even though it involves a 60-mile bus trip into an adjacent state when all of her friends are sleeping in on Sunday mornings. These types of characteristics make it all the more important for parents to develop a "battle plan" to assist their children with their learning disorders. They are worth the extra work and the extra financial sacrifice. God can use them in mighty ways.

Another part of the battle plan is finding the right strategy to use at home to help ensure the success of your child. Every child is unique, so your solutions will have a distinct flavor to them. For example, many of the strategies used by Dennis and Lauree with Dusty would not have been successful if used with Danielle.

Danielle was absolutely useless if she did not get enough sleep at night when she was in high school, so Diane helped her plan her schedule so that on most school evenings she got at least eight hours of sleep. Sometimes this meant creative solutions, like making a bed in the backseat of the car when coming home from a nighttime soccer game. But this worked in the Passno family to help her achieve her goals.

Dusty, on the other hand, responds to structure in routine and negative consequences if he departs from that structure. Now that Dusty is in his late teens, he must get up on his own, shower, dress, make his bed, and clean up his room before leaving the house. Otherwise, no truck, no jeep, no fun weekends. He does best in school when the teacher gives him structure as well: worksheets with expectations, clear due dates for assignments, and so forth.

Both Danielle and Dusty are fascinated by, and quite adept at, the computer. This seems to be characteristic of many children with ADHD: The computer keeps them focused, entertained, and occupied! They are much less distracted when using a computer than reading a book. If you can afford a computer for your home, we would highly recommend the purchase. If not, many schools have computer labs that students can access after hours, as do many public libraries.

Dennis and Lauree also tried another "technological" experiment that worked with Dusty, although it has been a complete failure with Danielle: the cell phone. The Swanbergs have given Dusty a cell phone with voicemail so that they can remind him to retrieve what he has forgotten at home: his backpack, shoulder pads, books—things he "stepped over" on the way to the car! (Can you hear Dennis grinding his teeth about now?) This technique doesn't work with Danielle because she forgets to turn the cell phone on, and her message box is so full of ignored voicemail that it won't accept any more words! Again, every parent must experiment to see what works for their ADHD child, and then use that technique to help them succeed.

The Swanbergs and the Passnos are in agreement about one solution: the use of appropriate rewards for behavior that you want repeated! Rewards don't have to be material in nature; words of praise and encouragement are all the reward that is necessary at times. However, Dusty's motivation to do well in school is spelled out in two words: JEEP and FOOTBALL. Danielle thrives on competition, so every assignment is a race to be won. A good grade on a paper is what excites her, even now as a college senior! So think about what works with your child, and don't think of using rewards as bribery. Rather, think of them as a technique to build your child up to reach the potential the Lord has built into his or her genetic code!

Lessons Learned

1. Always remember: The Lord loves your ADHD kid even more than you do, and He is in the business of answering your prayers for your child.
2. Obtaining good medical advice and competent pediatric assistance is very important. Your child needs help to survive the early years, even if he is home schooled.
3. ADHD children thrive with encouragement. They may be natural encouragers themselves, and many identify strongly with the underdog in social situations.
4. Many ADHD children are very open to the gospel and seem to have a hunger for things spiritual that other children in the family may not exhibit.
5. ADHD children are individuals, so solutions in the home to help them succeed will need to be "custom made" to fit their unique personalities and giftedness.

Reflection

Dennis and Diane: We know that you are concerned about your child's future, if only because you have picked up this book to read! Way back in the third chapter, Danielle expressed her heartache at the number of ADHD children in school who have been overlooked by everybody, never to be able to capitalize on the unique set of gifts that make them special. According to Dr. Bill Maier, "Individuals with ADHD are more likely to drop out of school, to have few or no friends, to have problems at work, to engage in antisocial activities, and to experience depression. They are also more prone to drug abuse, to experience teen pregnancy and sexually transmitted diseases, and to speed excessively and have multiple car accidents." He goes on to add, "Yet less than half of those with the disorder are receiving treatment. This is tragic!"

Questions for Parents

Do you have a success strategy in place for your child? At church? At school? At home? Have you involved yourself in this plan, or have you left it up to others to see that your child has a chance to move forward with confidence rather than backward with despair? Does your child know you believe in him and what he can achieve?

For you created my inmost being; you knit me together in my mother's womb. I praise you because I am fearfully and wonderfully made; your works are wonderful, I know that full well. My frame was not hidden from you when I was made in the secret place. When I was woven together in the depths of the earth, your eyes saw my unformed body. All the days ordained for me were written in your book before one of them came to be. (Psalm 139:13-16)

7

School Daze

One of the greatest worries of a child with ADD is
about his intellect. He should be given an IQ test and
have his high scores shown to him. Parents cannot
convince a child he is intelligent if he is failing in
school. . . . It is usually because he cannot prove
his intelligence with the pencil.
—NED OWENS, M.ED.[1]

School is generally where one can't help but see ADHD as a
disability. Where is the hope for ADHD students? One of the
things parents would do well to remember is that often it's
just a matter of changing the educational approach to utilize
the positives of ADHD. Again, the best way to level the playing field is to allow your child's skills to be used and developed. ADHD becomes an advantage when a parent makes
the effort to fit the child's unique world.

Diane: Danielle was fortunate in that she did not have
the horrific time in school that many children with ADHD
experience. I don't know if it was because of her high IQ,
wonderful teachers, or just plain luck, or maybe for all of
these factors. However, it is far more common for children
with ADHD to experience trauma when introduced to formal
education. These kids often give the appearance of being

unhappy or very nervous and anxious when they arrive at school in the morning.

Surprisingly, neither Dennis nor I fault teachers for their inability to manage this type of child perfectly. Thankfully, there are wonderful men and women out there who still want to make the world a better place for our kids by becoming teachers.

One of my friends, Joan Wooten, is married to the Senior Director of Counseling at Focus on the Family. She is a second grade teacher—the kind of teacher every parent would wish for their child. While on a hike with me in the woods one day, she described the success she had had in the classroom with a young boy with ADHD. I asked her to write down her observations, and they are so much in agreement with what Dennis and I recommend for parents that we wanted to share them with you:

> Having a child in class who has been diagnosed with ADHD does not have to be a threat or a frustration to a teacher. It is definitely true, however, that a teacher needs to have a basic understanding about ADHD: that ADHD is a developmental difference, that it appears with a variety of symptoms, that it is not the result of poor parenting, that it can be managed within the classroom in most cases. Teachers need to be educated about simple, practical techniques to use when working with an ADHD child that foster self-confidence and generate hope in the heart of a struggling student.
>
> A gently persistent and informed mother a few years ago awoke me to her son's needs when he first entered our school. She wrote me a personal, insightful letter about her son and included a book on ADHD in which she had highlighted simple modifications and accommodations that would help him to have less frustration and more success in the classroom. She knew him and his

needs well, and as we teamed up together to provide the best working environment, reasonable expectations, and structure for him, he began to be more engaged, motivated, and connected to his classmates. Mom was his best advocate and cheerleader, frustrated at times, but always believing he could be a winner. Parents need to do that for their ADHD kids, and teachers need to listen and learn from what they have to say.

Many of the ADHD children that have come through my class over the years have been bright, verbal, funny, delightfully creative youngsters who were desperately trying to deal with academic and/or social insecurities. Being overwhelmed with too much input at one time, unable to stay focused long enough to complete assignments, having trouble remembering or following a sequence of directions, having difficulty organizing thoughts in order to answer a question, or just trying to find a pencil, were merely a few of the roadblocks these ADHD children faced daily. My heart would go out to these "lost" students, and I would find myself moved to do whatever I could to ensure their success while encouraging them to cope and work with their differences. Sometimes all it takes is for a teacher to believe in a child's ability to be successful in order for that child to truly experience success.

Dennis: It's true! A parent and teacher teaming together to help a child with ADHD makes all the difference in the world. If an ADHD kid knows a teacher likes him, he can go to the moon! But he'll get into trouble if he senses that a teacher doesn't like him. These kids work best with someone who is calm and steady. If they know someone believes in them, they will give everything to that person. They remember kindness from teachers, believe me. Someone once said that rules without relationships lead to rebellion. An ADHD kid won't rebel if he has a relationship with his teacher, but if there are only rules, then there are problems.

I had a speech professor at Baylor University who had a real impact on my life because he was such an encourager. Dr. George Stokes could see my future as a public speaker. He gave me a B on every speech I wrote because of my poor grammar, but it didn't matter to me because he gave me hope. I think that's the reason my favorite Bible verse is Hebrews 10:25: "Let us not give up meeting together, as some are in the habit of doing, but let us encourage one another—and all the more as you see the Day approaching." So many Christians engage in what they call "constructive criticism," but it gets old fast. What I needed as a student struggling with ADHD was encouragement. A person can "feed" on one encouraging remark all day long! ADHD kids get enough criticism in one school year to last a lifetime. Dr. Stokes helped me change my attitude about myself.

Diane: One of Danielle's best friends is a graduate of Dartmouth College who now has a distinguished career with a well known national accounting firm. When Athena was visiting us one day, I told her a little about this book project. She confided to me that she had been diagnosed with ADHD after her first year of college. Her mother had pressured her in high school to be tested, but she had resisted the suggestion. However, in college she had experienced the same frustrations as Danielle, and began to realize that her style of learning and taking tests was very different from the other students in her classes.

"Tell me about it!" I asked. "What do you remember about elementary school?"

Athena proceeded to sit cross-legged on our sofa and pound out on her laptop a poignant, four-page story of her childhood memories about her experiences in school, not all of them positive. But one teacher handled her beautifully:

In third grade, I had a teacher, Mrs. Walther, who taught the way I learned. She let me do 15 things at once, and she even rewarded me for it. I remember her class like it was yesterday because it made me love learning. I could learn how I needed to learn, which in the process made me feel invincible. I look back at my awards scrapbook for elementary school, and I am most proud of the awards that I received in her class because I felt that I really deserved them, and I enjoyed earning them. The one that I am most proud of is the one that I received because I was "Child of the Year." I hadn't received this award because I had scored the highest on an exam or because I had behaved the best, but because I had received the most stars on the project board. I had obtained the most stars because I had successfully completed the most projects that year. In essence, she rewarded me for doing 15 things at once and learning outside the box of the classroom. I loved doing these projects because it meant I didn't have to sit still and do nothing. Mrs. Walther planned her classroom so that we were always busy. When I finished one task, I had another to move to. She kept my mind engaged.

Dennis: I like Athena's story because her teacher taught at her "success level" rather than at her "frustration level." She made Athena feel special, and she understood her learning style. I know it's a challenge to sometimes actually like the most difficult kid in the class, but there are such rewards if the effort is made. These kids are so filled with self-contempt because they feel that *they* are the problem, rather than the teaching method.

Athena had her best teacher in the third grade, but, as you've already read, my third grade experience was the opposite. For years I didn't have my third grade teacher on my list of folks who have influenced my life. But in hindsight, she was a good lady, a Christian. She was all business and didn't enjoy the silly stuff, but her class was my turning point. It was where I started to use my gifts to compensate for my inadequacies. She died a year or so ago. My mom called and told me. Mom said that she would bump into this teacher at the mall on occasion, and she would tell my mom how proud she was of my success. Little did she know that she was the catalyst for my comedic development.

The school system, whether it be public or private, is really not geared for the kid with ADHD, so these children have to work harder just to cope with the everyday classroom. It's like hearing a different language when everybody else is hearing English. They often need help with their social skills, their manners, their ability to interact with others, and their ability to control impulsive words and actions. But if a teacher has the patience to work with them, they have the potential to become extremely compassionate, conscientious, and considerate human beings.

Diane: My oldest daughter, Nicole, is an elementary school teacher with the patience of a saint. Perhaps she should thank her sister for preparing her for her career! She spent the first two years of her elementary teaching experience in the inner city. Many of the children came to school hungry, so she provided food out of her small salary. One child was particularly ingenious about the way he washed his clothes every week. He would come to the school on Saturdays when he knew the sprinklers would be on watering the grass, and that was his water supply for his laundry. So when a teacher is simply trying to meet the basic needs of the children entrusted to his or her care, it is often difficult to give the one-on-one attention that a child with a disability needs so desperately. However, the educational environment that you select for your ADHD child is arguably as important as the medical assistance you seek.

Nicole has had many children with ADHD in her classrooms, and in addition, she has been a nanny for a wonderful little boy with ADHD. She has had unusual success with these children and she offers these suggestions, not only for teachers, but parents as well:

- These children seem to focus best in an organized, structured environment with clear expectations and rules that have consistent consequences and rewards.
- These kids seem to follow directions best when there are no more than three to five steps to follow.
- I always offer a warning before enforcing a consequence.
- I always have specific places in my classroom for different activities, so there is a lot of structured movement for the children, and they know what to expect when they are in a specific area. For example, there is a spot where they can snack, a place where they can read, and a place where they can do homework.
- I also have specific tasks associated with specific times during the day and evening. The kids know what to expect at a certain time, and they like that type of predictability and schedule.
- I try to give these children lots of tasks to do for me that give them a sense of importance and responsibility. It is very empowering for them to have chores with which they are trusted, like taking care of the class pet or taking notes to the office.
- These children love the opportunity to earn rewards, like an allowance for doing specific chores in the home, or stickers for completing their homework. I spend a lot of money on little prizes that they can earn with "good behavior points"!
- These children love fun and they love to be motivated. I create a lot of activities that are hands-on for them, as well as ones that are of high interest to a particular child. This takes a lot of extra work, but the children seem to thrive on it, so the time is well spent.

- These children need breaks when they are asked to do activities that are tedious. Sometimes, activities have to be modified for them because they simply can't sit still long enough to do what the other children in class are doing.
- Most of all, be patient with ADHD kids. I try to communicate with them more intensely than the other children. I also try to keep good communication between all the adults who are working with the child and the parents, so that he is making progress rather than becoming discouraged or embarrassed by his learning style.

Danielle makes this point to reinforce the items on her sister's list: "ADHD kids are always being told by adults, especially teachers, to 'sit down and pay attention,' but do they understand how hard this is to do—how hard it is to sit through a 30-minute video? You get in trouble when you yell out answers in class, regardless of whether the answer is correct, because the teacher considers your social actions inappropriate. Sometimes you just want to dig a hole in the ground and disappear, you're so embarrassed."

Dr. Bill Maier suggests that parents have a dialogue with their child's teacher that goes somewhat like this: "I know my child is having difficulties in your classroom and can sometimes be disruptive. I'm hoping we can work together to help my child succeed academically and socially. If you will communicate with me on a regular basis, I'm willing to follow through with consequences at home. I will do my best to provide rewards for positive classroom behavior and negative consequences for disruptive behavior."

He adds, "Most teachers will appreciate your attitude and your offer to help. My wife is a second grade teacher and typically has one or two ADHD children in her classroom each year. She is able to help these children best when their parents are involved and willing to cooperate in the educational process. On the other hand, if your son's or daughter's teacher is completely uncooperative, refuses to acknowledge your child's ADHD, and simply sees him or her as a 'bad seed,' I would recommend an immediate conference with the principal and the school psychologist."

Diane: In one of her engineering courses at Dartmouth, Danielle was on a team that was given the assignment to build a car. The professor had constructed an obstacle course, and the grade for the class was based upon whether the car was able to negotiate the course. One of the difficulties was building a car that could negotiate the curves in the valleys on the course, and Danielle's team was finding that task particularly daunting. Danielle, because of her ability to think creatively, came up with the idea of building the car to go over the hills rather than through the valleys. Their car passed with flying colors!

Dennis: I've always been easily distracted. It's really difficult for me to concentrate on just one thing—I love juggling a lot of things all at once. But I'm a prime example of what happens when you give kids with ADHD a chance. I know I have always thought differently from others—I knew that from my first year in school. But I have a lot of gifts, and one

---

What about home schooling for ADHD youngsters?
Dr. Larimore: For many kids with learning difficulties, home schooling can be a very useful intervention—especially for the parents who are dedicated to doing this and willing to do what they need to do. I have talked to many doctors of ADHD patients who relate countless examples of kids who have done much better when they've shifted to a home school environment. But be aware, home schooling is not for every parent or every child, so don't feel bad if you decide it's not for your family.

of them is speaking. I talk to thousands of people every year and make them laugh, just like I made my teachers laugh. I champion the underdog, even when I do it with humor, because I know how it feels to be different and to struggle. When people come and hear me speak, I want the words of encouragement I bring to give hope to the hurting and point them to God, who was my Source of encouragement when things looked the bleakest when I was a kid in school.

Lessons Learned

1. ADHD children are often very vulnerable, and a teacher who understands their unique styles of learning will make a tremendous difference in their development and self-image. It is imperative for parents and teachers to work together for the benefit of an ADHD child.
2. Not all teachers understand ADHD or have patience with this type of child in the classroom. Talk with other parents of ADHD kids to find which teachers handle these kids well, then request the teacher you think will best suit your child.
3. Each child has to eventually find techniques that work for him or her. Whether it is reading alone in a quiet place or being tested apart from the other students in the classroom, these kids do not learn the way other children do, and alternatives need to be considered.
4. Remember, it isn't "lowering the bar" to adjust the standards to fit the decidedly different learning style of ADHD students. This is the only way many children will ever see ADHD as an advantage rather than a disability.

Reflection

Dennis: Jesus Christ modeled for us the perfect Teacher. He used different techniques to reach different audiences. In some situations, as when he was with Mary and Martha, he was loving and patient. To other audiences, He showed His

deity and authority by His use of miracles, like the multiply-
ing of the loaves and fishes. And to still others, He was force-
ful and direct, as when He spoke to the Pharisees and
Sadducees prior to His arrest and crucifixion. He used stories
to convey powerful messages to His audiences. In other
words, He did not employ just one teaching style to fit every
situation. He knew how uniquely different He had made His
creation! And He never flew off the handle when His disciples didn't understand. He merely changed His approach.

Diane: One of the best examples of this would be when
Jesus spoke to the woman at the well (John 4:1-26). He
crossed all cultural barriers to reach this woman, and as a
result, she heard the message of who He was and that she
was truly forgiven for her sins—that she had a new life made
possible by her Creator God. If the Lord used different methods to reach different people, it is simply logical to assume
that there are different educational choices that every parent
can consider for their children. We have already discussed
the public school scenario, but there are also private and
Christian school options, as well as home schooling.

Questions for Parents

The Lord made your ADHD child a rare, very special individual. No one else on the planet is like him! Have you considered all educational options available to him to ensure his
future success? If he is in school, what is your relationship
with his teacher? Remember: Your concerns about your child
are not too big for an all-powerful God!

> *The LORD is righteous in all his ways and loving
> toward all he has made. The LORD is near to all who
> call on him, to all who call on him in truth. He fulfills
> the desires of those who fear him; he hears their cry
> and saves them. The LORD watches over all who love
> him.* (Psalm 145:17-20A)

8

Brothers, Sisters, and Parents

Fear not, for I have redeemed you; I have summoned you
by name; you are mine. When you pass through the
waters, I will be with you; and when you pass through
the rivers, they will not sweep over you. When you walk
through the fire, you will not be burned; the flames will
not set you ablaze. For I am the LORD, your God, the
Holy One of Israel, your Savior.
—ISAIAH 43:1B-3B

Diane: My husband and I could not have raised Danielle with any semblance of sanity but for the help of her sister, Nicole. I don't think we are peculiar in this regard, and yet parents of ADHD children are usually too tired and stressed out to recognize the assistance they get from their other children who are "normal." So much of their attention is focused on the ADHD child out of necessity. Now that we have an empty nest and the time to reflect, we feel a tinge of guilt for the number of times we leaned on Nicole for her patience and methodical way of relating to her younger sister.

When Nicole was about 10, and Danielle five, I was in

the kitchen cooking dinner when I realized we were out of milk. The kids were engrossed in some game in the family room, and I debated whether to bundle them up for a trip to the market, particularly when I would be gone no more than 10 minutes. I called Nicole into the bathroom while I ran a brush through my hair.

"Honey, would you please watch Sisty for just a few minutes? I want to dash to the store. Do you think you could do this, or would you rather come with me?"

Nicole readily agreed to the assignment. But what came next was the shocker: Within a couple of minutes—the time it took me to freshen my lipstick and pull on a sweater—Nicole had reappeared with a diagram on a sheet of paper. She had outlined the escape routes from the home in case

---

What are some ways ADHD affects marriage and parenting?

Dr. Larimore: ADHD is not a problem that affects only the person living with it. The time and effort required to deal with ADHD can significantly disrupt the entire family.

In most families, it is the mother who has the greatest emotional, relational, and spiritual risk in caring for an ADHD child. Although these kids can be intensely loving, they can also turn on their moms in a second. They can at times be verbally or emotionally abusive to their parents, which can wound parents deeply. They can be wonderful one day and horrible the next—or they can change from hour to hour.

Moms of ADHD kids need to quickly give up the delusion that their homes will be immaculate or that every meal will be a joyous family affair. ADHD parents have to quickly learn that they are not perfect and that they may need help. Not only can they be rejected and hurt by their child, these parents may have to face the dislike, hostility, or animosity of other parents or neighbors. They may have to deal with seeing their child rejected by other children and adults.

there was an emergency or a fire in my absence. I was dumb-founded! Is it any wonder we "leaned" on this child a bit more than we should have in bringing up Danielle? She was always thinking ahead . . . and was eminently trustworthy.

I used to refer to Nicole as "the perfect child" because she was in so many ways. I didn't realize until later in life that Danielle had as much a "whirlwind" impact on her as she did on her father and me. Danielle received so much of our attention that Nicole got used to being taken for granted.

One of my precious memories is of Danielle, tears streaming unchecked down her cheeks, saying good-bye to her sister as Nicole left home for college. Danielle admitted later that she thought the family would have no more fun with Nicole gone. Their rooms were across the hall from each

---

The ADHD child may be physically aggressive and must be taught to convert physical aggression into verbal expression (a skill some adults need to gain as well). The ADHD child is not uncommonly verbally abusive. Once again, learning how to teach your child to redirect this behavior into constructive behavior is essential. Parents of ADHD kids quickly learn that they cannot force or coerce their kids to be like "normal" kids—they will never fit into that mold. They are wired differently and their parents need to learn a wide variety of parenting skills to cope with, teach, train, and creatively discipline these unique kids.

These stresses, along with others, can wreck many marriages. Therefore, I feel it is critical that parents of ADHD kids get counseling. The parenting skills needed for ADHD kids are different from those that work with kids without ADHD, but these skills can be learned. Also, being in a support group with other parents of ADHD kids can be wonderful, especially if the parents share your faith convictions.

other, and for months after her sister left, Danielle chose to sleep upstairs, close to her father and me. Nicole had been her confidante and protector, and it took almost a year for Danielle to adjust to her absence.

As I mentioned before, Nicole was the one who packed for her sister before trips; she was the one who fixed her hair for occasions that called for more than a ponytail; she was the one who taught her the "rules"—the "unspoken code of conduct" for school, especially when it came to relating to her peers. She was a role model for Danielle, and in so many ways was the one who taught her how to "get her act together."

When Danielle lacked the patience for the repetition involved in practicing piano in preparation for her weekly lessons, Nicole would sit with her and patiently go through the assignment with her hour by hour, week by week. When Danielle was too flighty to read a lengthy book for a book report, Nicole taught her how to skim pages and take notes on what she had read. Danielle admired her big sister so much that she tried to emulate the way she did everything, even though it was contrary to her very nature. And not a night went by in those growing-up years when her father and I didn't hear those wonderful words, "Good night, Sisty! I love you!" And the response, "I love you too, Sister!"

The Scripture verses at the beginning of this chapter are no mistake. Dennis and Lauree and Paul and I feel so strongly that siblings are God's hands and feet in keeping their ADHD brothers and sisters walking a straight line, clear of trouble—especially when they are out of sight of their parents in the school setting. If they are older, they serve as their protectors, and the recipients of that love and safekeeping are forever grateful.

Dennis: Dusty will call his brother, Chad, before anybody else if he is in trouble. Chad and Dusty are three years apart, yet Chad has always let Dusty tag along with him and his friends, even when he was being a pain in the neck. There is

probably a great Bible study here about the relationship between brothers and friends.

Andrew brought Simon Peter to Jesus, and although Andrew was less flamboyant than his brother, he could be called Christianity's first missionary. Yet one never reads that Andrew was jealous of the role that Jesus gave to his brother as the rock of the church. The Old Testament recounts the wonderful account of Jonathan, Saul's oldest son and rightful heir, who befriended a shepherd boy named David. He always put David's interests in front of his own, and even saved his life, yet was never disloyal to his father. In another Old Testament story, we learn of Joshua, whom God gave the honor of leading the children of Israel into the Promised Land. Caleb, by right of seniority, should have been given that honor, yet he subordinated himself to the Lord's selection. And then there was Barnabas, a respected Levite, who was instrumental in bringing the newly converted Saul to respectability in the eyes of the apostles in Jerusalem. Think about it! There are a dozen or so examples in Scripture of one worthy individual subordinating his personal interests for those of another. In many ways, siblings of ADHD kids play much the same role in a family. They often become the "lesser" so that more attention can be focused on the child with the problem.

Chad always seemed to cover for Dusty when he was in trouble. But I can remember one time when the roles were reversed and Dusty stood up for his big brother. Chad got into trouble once in high school, and as a result, was suspended from playing in two football games. He was really upset about it. Well, I took the family out to eat at this catfish place, and after we had ordered our food, I made a caustic remark about Chad's behavior.

"Boy, oh boy. I hope you had a really good time with those friends of yours because you've embarrassed your mama and me real good, Son. You should know better! We raised you better! Where were your brains, Boy? And your team was counting on you! What kind of example are you, anyway?"

Dusty got tears in his eyes during my tirade, and got up to go to the restroom. As he left the table, he looked at me and said, "I don't care what my brother does. I love him!" That shut me up real quick. It showed me in no uncertain terms the bonding that had occurred between the boys over the years.

Dusty has always looked up to Chad, and for good reason. Chad is extremely intelligent and an unbelievable overcomer. Chad has always had to fight asthma and he's allergic to everything, which has really been a struggle, especially as a college athlete. All this to say that Chad has had to overcome a lot to be what he is today. He plays football for Mississippi College as a defensive back and tailback, and Lauree and I are proud of what he has accomplished, both scholastically and athletically.

Well, a couple of years ago, a confrontation occurred between Chad and Dusty that had a dramatic impact on Dusty's life. Despite the three years between them, the younger brother outweighs the older by about 30 pounds, even though they are the same height. Now this wouldn't matter much, except that Dusty's extra weight is such an advantage to him. The problem was, Dusty, who doesn't have asthma and is so strong that he's on the State Power Lifting Team, was just throwing his athletic talent away because of his ADHD. He had so much potential but it was going down the drain.

He was misunderstood by his coaches because of the difficulty he has paying attention. Dusty simply wasn't responding to their instructions, or their yelling, or their disciplinary measures. He started to make excuses to them and to me. He began to think that they didn't like him, and so Dusty became indolent and uninterested in football, even though he had the talent to play.

Well, big brother Chad noticed what was happening—
that Dusty was lazy and playing the blame game, so he went
up to the sports field house and took him right off the field in
the middle of practice! He had a face-to-face confrontation:
"Swanbergs give it everything they've got, and you're a
Swanberg. We work out hard, and we don't take the easy way
out of things. We pay attention and we don't complain. Now,
you get out there and be a Swanberg, and don't let anyone
ever say that a Swanberg is lazy or whiny or a complainer!"

Dusty respects his big brother so much that he turned
around and went into the weight room and started doing
squat repetitions on the weights. Heavy duty, nonstop. And
then he went outside and ran and did "bear crawls." He was
never the same after that! He is now a hard working lineman
and a hard-nosed weight lifter who came in fourth in state
competition this year. And it's all because his big brother
stepped into his life with a tough love message and a challenge. If that same challenge had been given by a coach or
even by me, his dad, I don't think it would have mattered as
much. Big brother made all the difference in the world.

Chad calls Dusty regularly from college and tells him he
loves him and believes in him. Here Chad, the A student, is
encouraging his little brother, the ADHD student who struggles to make B's and C's and often has to settle for D's. Dusty
says he gets those calls just when he needs them. So often
when he's depressed and struggling with academics, the
phone rings and it's Chad. Those calls are what make it possible for Dusty to get through another day at school. It's
because his big brother believes in him.

Brothers and sisters of ADHD kids have every right to ask
their parents, "Hey! What about me?" We spent so much time
with Dusty taking him to tutoring, learning centers, and
teacher's conferences, that he was going through life as the
"little kingpin" of the family. Our lives revolved around him.

I think there is an analogy to the lesson in Scripture about the prodigal son (Luke 15:11-32). In that parable, the good son who did everything right was not the one who received the best robe and the fattened calf. He served his father day in and day out, yet the focus of the celebration was his younger brother, who squandered his share of the inheritance and returned home a broken man. Although this is a beautiful parable of God's treatment of sinners, I think parents have to remember the "good children" at home who may *appear* to not need as much attention as their ADHD brother or sister, but in many ways need just as much. It's as exhausting for them to be in a household with one of these kids as it is for the parents.

Diane and Dennis: One of the neat outcomes for the kind of relationship that Dusty and Danielle have had with Chad and Nicole is that they are wonderful "mentors" themselves when it comes to working with younger kids. They learned firsthand from their siblings how to "be there" for kids who

---

What effect does living with an ADHD child have on siblings?
Dr. Larimore: The ADHD child can make their siblings' lives miserable. Not all do, of course, but many are difficult to live with. Consequently, medical studies are beginning to show that siblings can also be at risk of emotional problems. These siblings can be chronically victimized by the ADHD child, who can bully them, verbally abuse them, physically abuse them, and, overall, be intense, demanding, and obnoxious to them.

Further, if siblings do not receive the attention and time that they need and deserve because that time is diverted to the ADHD child, they can feel alienated, rejected, or unloved. These feelings can lead to a whole slew of behavioral problems, especially in adolescence. Therefore, many ADHD care providers will recommend that siblings be part of the family counseling. The good news is that the skills these siblings will gain will be helpful to them for life.

may be underdogs. For example, Dusty has a great relationship with a 10-year-old neighbor boy, and has really come into his own in the role of mentor. Danielle has taught a program called Summerbridge for children who need that extra push to succeed in school. We believe that Dusty and Danielle have a heart for people because of the healthy relationships they had with their older brother and sister.

Lessons Learned

1. ADHD impacts an entire family, not just the child with ADHD.
2. Brothers and sisters of these children need nurturing and attention from their parents as much as their siblings do.
3. Parents need to be careful not to place too much responsibility on the "normal kids" in the family, so much so that the ADHD child is excused from responsible behavior.

Reflection

Diane: One of my all-time favorite books is Louisa May Alcott's *Little Women*. I have copies of two different versions of it on video, and every time I watch either version, I cry buckets of tears over the death of little Beth. I think what I love best about the book is the wonderful relationship the March sisters shared despite their uniquely different personalities and gifts. The relationship between sisters Martha and Mary in the Gospels of Luke and John is equally fascinating to me. It is reminiscent of the relationship I had with my younger sister, and my tendency to always take control, whether my sister wanted me to or not. Shades of Martha! Although it is plain that Jesus loved both women, it is surprising to someone of my "bent" to know that there are aspects of my personality that might be considered grating, rather than beneficial!

Since the onslaught of the empty nest, I have had more time to ponder . . . to think back on the type of relationship Nicole and Danielle had with each other when they were growing up. It surprises me how similar it is to the relationship I had with my sister. In hindsight, I do think I put too much pressure on Nicole to help her little sister through the rough spots in school. True, they have a wonderful adult relationship, but I think I would have handled some situations differently if I had to do it all over again. For example, Danielle's athletics took so much of the family time. It never occurred to me that Nicole might not enjoy it as much as we did, even though she never complained about accompanying us to a thousand and one games.

Dennis: I guess every parent has to live with some regrets. We don't want our kids to experience the same pain we endured when we were kids, and so we often overcompensate in one way or another. I think the key is BALANCE. Just as God our Father models the perfect balance of love and justice to His people, we too have to find balance in the way we relate to our children. I don't think any of us can look back on our lives and not have something we would do differently if we had a chance to repeat history. None of us wants to be guilty of giving one child in the family more attention than the other child or children.

Question for Parents

Have you taken an objective look at the kids in your family lately? Sometimes it takes seemingly every ounce of energy we possess as parents to simply meet their day-to-day physical needs. However, taking inventory—healthy soul-searching—can be so helpful in discovering whether you have perhaps overlooked the needs of a quiet, submissive child in order to deal with a brother or sister whose behavior is more demanding.

Brothers, Sisters, and Parents

This is how we know what love is: Jesus Christ laid down his life for us. And we ought to lay down our lives for our brothers. . . . Dear children, let us not love with words or tongue but with actions and in truth. (1 John 3:16, 18)

9

ADHD: BC and AD

*There are many positives with ADD, including
a surplus of ideas, creativity, excitement, and
interest which accompany this kind of mind.*
—SARI SOLDEN[1]

Before winding down with our part of this tome and letting
Dr. Walt have his turn with the pen, we simply couldn't
resist having a little fun with one chapter! Many of you will
think this is a "stretch," but we feel that there is evidence of
many a Bible hero having some of the characteristics of
ADHD. Bear with us while we speculate!

Dennis read somewhere that the German literary giant
Goethe, author of the epic poem *Faust,* thought that there
were 33 different kinds of situations in life in which people
may become involved, and that he had found 32 of those
situations reflected in the pages of Scripture. All this to say
that the Bible is a picture gallery of every sort of human
predicament, and we can still learn from the lives of our
biblical heroes centuries after the fact. We will look at the
lives of four men in Scripture: some stumbled because of
their ADHD characteristics; others triumphed in spite of
them!

MOSES

Moses was a mighty man of God who is referenced in many books of the Bible. He was first a prince of Egypt, later a shepherd in the wilderness, and finally, God's agent to deliver the Hebrews from slavery in Egypt. He was by nature impulsive. One day, when he observed an Egyptian beating a Hebrew slave, he impetuously struck and killed the Egyptian. Forced to flee the court of Egypt, he escaped to Midian, where he married into the family of Jethro, the priest. Most of us have read about the personality characteristics of Moses as recorded in Scripture: Not only was he impetuous, but he was reluctant to follow the instructions of the Lord when He commissioned him to return to Pharaoh to request the freedom of his people. He was full of excuses, even going so far as to blame his inability to move forward on his speech defect, a tendency to stammer. The Lord used him in magnificent ways, despite his human flaws. However, Moses' tendency to act impulsively cost him the honor of being the one to bring the Hebrews into the Promised Land.

In Numbers 20:8-13 we read the sad story. Moses seemed to have suffered from what some with ADHD call a "blink." It was a moment when he simply spaced out and overlooked the very thing that God had told him to do. God had stated very clearly that Moses was to speak to the rock in order to bring forth water for the people and their livestock, but Moses "went Hollywood" and dramatically struck the rock twice to effect the miracle. God had little patience for that, and judgment was passed.

Lessons Learned

There are always consequences when folks with impulsive tendencies disregard instructions and guidelines that others give them for their benefit. This is one reason why it is necessary to teach ADHD kids coping techniques that will help them curb their impetuousness, in order for this characteristic to be channeled for good rather than used for ill.

SAUL

Saul had such promise as the first king of Israel. We are told that he had everything going for him: He was energetic, courageous, and a great man of war who was blessed with the physical size to make him fearsome to the enemies of Israel, the Philistines. However, after his initial successes, character traits began to appear in him that were quite unpleasant, two of which were jealousy and the tendency for rashness. Eventually he had bouts with mental illness with outbursts of insanity. He died by committing suicide.

We read in 1 Samuel 18:10-11 that, after an evil spirit from God entered Saul, he threw his spear at David in a fit of jealousy. Again, in chapter 19, Saul attempts to kill or have David killed by his soldiers, all in vain. These episodes show the impetuous, jealous, and unstable nature of Saul—his capacity to change his mind and intent suddenly with inappropriate actions that have negative consequences for him and those around him. We cannot discount the Lord's historical purposes in allowing Saul to contend with bouts of insanity. What we can understand is that it was illogical, to say the least, for King Saul to keep trying to kill his son-in-law—one who was happily married to his daughter and who had been a loyal subject with no blemishes on his record. David had the giftedness and potential to bring glory to the reign of his father-in-law. Instead, Saul's impulsiveness and jealousy led to his destruction and death.

Lessons Learned

The lessons learned from the life of Saul are the same ones we learned from the life of Moses. Impetuous behavior spells disaster. Saul was in a position of authority, so the ramifications of his behavior had far-reaching consequences.

Impulsiveness can be devastating if it is not channeled appropriately. When this characteristic is paired with jealousy, all sorts of mischief is possible. And yet these two personality traits could very well be the reaction of an ADHD child in the classroom who is ridiculed by his peers because he is just a little out of step with everyone else. Think about it!

SIMON PETER

There is a television show titled, "Everybody Loves Raymond." Well, we think most everybody loves Simon Peter! His constant mistakes, his tendency to put his foot in his mouth, his ups and downs are so typical of the human condition. And yet the Lord built His church on the rock known as Peter! Jesus comprehended that Peter's weaknesses would also be his strengths if they were channeled for kingdom work.

In the sixth chapter of John, we learn that many of the followers of Christ left Him after His teaching about eating His flesh and drinking His blood. The Lord was not talking about cannibalism, but these men didn't stick around to understand what He meant. Jesus inquired of the Twelve if they wanted to hit the road as well. Peter then says these wonderful words, "Lord, to whom shall we go? You have the words of eternal life. We believe and know that you are the Holy One of God" (John 6:68-69).

Every time we read that passage, we love Peter for recognizing just who Jesus was! And yet this same man could be so exasperating that you cannot help but smile at some of the things he said and did. For example, when the transfiguration occurred as recorded in Matthew 17 and Moses and Elijah were talking with Jesus, Peter blurts out that it's a good thing he's along because he can build them three shelters! Is this a logical response to witnessing such a miracle?

In Matthew 26, Peter boasts that he will never leave Jesus, even if he has to die with Him. Yet before the night is over, he has fallen asleep in the Garden of Gethsemane within an hour after the Lord asked him to keep watch and pray, and he has fallen back asleep after being gently rebuked by Jesus (Matthew 26:40); he has cut off the ear of Malchus, the high priest's servant (John 18:10); and he has denied the Lord three times (Matthew 26:34). In the space of one night, he showed that he could be inattentive and impulsive, and would use cover-up when in a situation that was personally frightening.

Lessons Learned

Peter made constant mistakes, had to be rebuked frequently by Jesus, had boisterous and impetuous enthusiasm that was often inappropriate for the situation, and lacked courage when it mattered. However, the Lord used him in a mighty way to establish His church. What a wonderful lesson for anyone with ADHD! Despite our failures, the Lord can use lives yielded to Him in incredible ways!

JOHN MARK

John Mark wrote the Gospel of Mark, which many Bible scholars refer to as the most action packed of the four Gospels. Mark presents our Savior in constant action, His divinity revealed in miracle after miracle. Although Mark was not one of the twelve disciples, he did accompany Paul and Barnabas, his cousin, on their first mission trip (Acts 12: 25). However, at a critical time in the mission, he vacillated, lost his focus, and returned home prematurely. Paul was so disgusted with him that he told Barnabas he didn't want Mark along on their next trip (Acts 15:37-39). Barnabas and Paul disagreed so sharply over the matter that they parted company, and Mark accompanied Barnabas to Cyprus.

This is not a very auspicious beginning, is it? Mark seemed eager to do the right thing initially, but had trouble completing a task. What harm would it have done to stay with Paul and Barnabas until they were done with their trip? In the Gospel he authored, Mark mentions a young man who was so frightened during Jesus' arrest that he fled without his clothes, and many Bible scholars think Mark was talking about himself. Yet Barnabas had faith in the young man, and was a source of encouragement to him when he needed it the most. The result: God used Mark to further His kingdom, just as He used Simon Peter—despite all his mistakes!

Mark was later reconciled with Paul. ("Get Mark and bring him with you, because he is helpful to me in my ministry" 2 Timothy 4:11.) Mark and his mother opened their home as a meeting place for Christians living in Jerusalem, and he also redeemed himself on subsequent mission trips. And, of course, he did author one of the most beloved books in Scripture.

Lessons Learned

John Mark and Simon Peter show us that God is in the business of using frail human beings whose lives are fraught with mistakes for His purposes. Lives submitted to Christ, despite any disability, work to the glory of God. And as Dennis and I have maintained in previous chapters, a little encouragement to someone with ADHD goes a long, long way. What would Mark have accomplished if Barnabas had not believed in him and had not taken the time to mentor him? Mark learned from his mistakes, and the Lord was able to use him.

Reflection

Each of us can identify with someone we've read about in the Bible. The Lord can use anyone to accomplish His purposes. Our Creator God does not define us by our disabilities. ADHD children and adults are part of God's plan—He doesn't make mistakes.

Questions for Parents

Is there a Bible story about someone similar in nature to your child, who exemplifies how the Lord uses people for His glory? Would your child be encouraged by hearing that story?

> *If the LORD delights in a man's way, he makes his steps firm; though he stumble, he will not fall, for the LORD upholds him with his hand.* (Psalm 37:23-24)

10

Attention Deficit Dividends

ADD people are high energy and incredibly good brainstormers. They will often happily work 12 to 15 hours by choice. The business community should not fear ADD. Instead, they should see that they have a potential gold mine here.
—DR. KATHLEEN NADEAU, psychologist with ADHD, appearing on "ABC News"[1]

If you have been diagnosed as having ADHD, this chapter is for *you*! We want you to read these pages every time you have the desperate thought that you are not going to make it, that you don't fit in with the rest of the world, that you are one odd duck in a lake full of swans. These are the "rules for survival" for anyone with Attention Deficit, no matter the specific diagnosis.

Learn to Delegate

This is the key to success. You cannot change the way your brain functions, so learn to involve other people in your projects who have the gifts for detail and order that you lack. For example, Dennis has always been the visionary, the one with the creative dreams. But he employs a lot of people who take care of the details of making those dreams a reality. He has the fun part—entertaining folks all across the country. But he has an accountant, a manager, a road manager, and a scheduler. Most important of all, though, is Lauree, his wife

---

Does ADHD go away?

Dr. Larimore: Some researchers believe that ADHD may, for many, be a lifelong condition. But what do the medical studies actually show? One review of nine studies prospectively followed groups of children with ADHD into adolescence or early adulthood.[2] In one analysis, researchers demonstrated that ADHD symptoms do usually decrease over time— with the rate of the disorder dropping by about 50 percent every five years. Nevertheless, researchers found that between 22 to 85 percent of adolescents and 4 to 50 percent of adults that had ADHD in childhood continued to meet the criteria for its diagnosis. In other words, up to one-half of children with ADHD may carry it into their adult years.[3]

Many experts believe that ADHD may be the most common chronic undiagnosed mental health condition in adults. As it is in kids, adults with ADHD manifest inattention, easy distractibility, mood swings, quick tempers, impulsivity, restlessness, overactivity, and disorganization. However, severe attention problems are seen more often in adults with ADHD than in kids. The adult form of ADHD is as likely in women as men, whereas the childhood diagnosis is three to five times more common in boys. Good diagnostic tests are not yet available to definitely diagnose ADHD in adults. Nevertheless, the adult form of ADHD is said to always follow childhood ADHD.

So, those who do have ADHD have a real difference, without a doubt, and the parents or siblings or spouses or employers of people with this special condition have to deal with it.

---

and executive vice president of their ministry, who takes care of the details of his life so nothing gets dropped.

It's a Balancing Act

What makes you unique is your ability to juggle many tasks at the same time. You are like those acrobats who spin plates on tall poles. First one plate, then another, and another . . . and they are all spinning at the same time! Do you remember Danielle's friend Athena who was mentioned in chapter seven? She made it through college despite having ADHD, and writes:

> I am now working in the corporate world for a large consulting firm and having ADD has almost been a blessing! My work requires me to keep a high level of energy for sometimes as long as 12 hours a day and to be able to do 15 things at once. I have received outstanding evaluations for my ability to maintain a high level of energy while still remaining organized and for my ability to solve problems in the fast-paced business environment.

Guess what? That's what you can do too!

Make the Most of Your Creativity

Is your mind always dreaming, thinking of a new idea, or creating a new project? When you see a need or hear of a problem, does your mind kick into gear to solve it? You are an individual "Internet" with the potential for a million and one Web sites of your own invention. Your type of mind is what gives the world movies, great music, new inventions, and original ideas about the way to conduct business. So relish your creativity and continue to dream big dreams!

You Can Show Others a Huge Heart

You have the potential to love others and to empathize with their pain. Because your empathy is genuine, you have those qualities that endear you to others. You can be a very good friend. This is one area where your tendency to be easily distracted is a benefit, for you are more observant of what is happening around you and the emotions that others are feeling. Do you remember Danielle's experience on the bench in college softball? She knew she could play better than the other shortstop on the team, but God had a different plan for her: She was the encourager for all the girls who didn't get a chance to play.

You Have All the Ingredients to Be Successful

Don't be ashamed of your failures, for by facing them, you have taken the first step toward being successful in what you want to do. Don't hesitate to take the help offered by your parents, teachers, pastor, friends, supervisor, mentor, counselor, siblings, and others. ADHD kids need to learn how to live within the structure of their home and school. You have a lot to learn and many people who want desperately for you to succeed, so listen to their advice.

How can I learn to be more organized?

Dr. Larimore: For adults and teens with ADHD, learning to minimize distractibility and impulsivity is very helpful. You can learn to use to-do lists, daily calendars, schedules, and written plans. "It ain't easy," as they say, but it can be done.

Another step for adolescents or adults with ADHD is to secure the assistance of a coach or a mentor. This is a knowledgeable friend or parent who is available at the "sound of a whistle" to offer encouragement, point out mistakes, teach, and assist in modifying behavior. If a wise instructor can teach a novice to play tennis or golf, a caring coach can help a person with ADHD learn to behave in more successful ways.

Do You See the Big Picture?

Remember Dennis telling about his experience with Dusty at the Super Bowl? Dusty "saw what the blimp saw." Many people with ADHD share that characteristic. You see life through a different set of lenses than the rest of us, so rejoice in it! You have a better view of life than people who are so focused that they don't notice anything around them. You can see the rainbow God has painted across the sky after a thunderstorm, while others are only focused on the pavement. This ability allows you to problem solve in unique ways. You may be in the lower percentile when you take the SAT or ACT exams, but your mind does not follow the same set of rules as everybody else's. So don't get discouraged by test scores. There are many very talented people who have gone before you who've made it, despite the test scores. You're in good company.

Think Sports

Though it's not a hard and fast rule, many people with ADHD have great success in sports, whether in school or in recreation leagues. Sports and ADHD go together like hot fudge and vanilla ice cream because there is perpetual motion involved. The mind has to constantly refocus to keep up with the continuous activity involved so there is little opportunity for boredom. Dennis, Dusty, and Danielle have all been most at home on an athletic field because the environment fits their temperaments so perfectly. That is not to say, however, that everyone with ADHD is a natural athlete. If you are not, you may enjoy walking, running, hiking, or other leisure sports in which you can use up some of your energy, yet not worry about being especially coordinated or competitive.

Lessons Learned

Always remember that God knew exactly what He was doing when He created you. *And God doesn't make mistakes.* You are a very special individual. Don't ever forget that!

Reflection

If Scripture teaches us anything, it is that God can use anybody at any time for His purposes. He is the Great Encourager and Redeemer. He is in the business of using each one of us for wonderful purposes.

A Question for Anyone with ADHD

Do I really believe the Lord has a plan for my life?

"For I know the plans I have for you," declares the LORD, "plans to prosper you and not to harm you, plans to give you hope and a future. Then you will call upon me and come and pray to me, and I will listen to you. You will seek me and find me when you seek me with all your heart." (Jeremiah 29:11-13)

Q & A with Dr. Larimore

In my opinion, the ADD brain structure is not truly an abnormality. In fact, I believe a very good case can be made that it is not only normal, though in the minority, but may well be a superior brain structure. However, the talents of the person with ADD brain structure are not those rewarded by our society in its current stage of development. In other words, the problems of the person with ADD are caused as much by the way we have our society, educational system, and the business methods organized as by other factors more directly related to the ADD itself.

—PAUL ELLIOTT, M.D.[1]

Diane and Dennis: As we've told our stories, we hope you've gained encouragement and perhaps some new ways to relate to your ADHD child. We are parents of kids with ADHD, but we aren't doctors. We know you probably have further questions about the behavioral and medical sides of this condition. That's why we've asked Dr. Walt Larimore, vice president of medical outreach at Focus on the Family and a practicing family physician of over 20 years, to answer a few

of the questions parents commonly ask about ADHD. So . . .
the doctor is in!

What causes ADHD?
We simply do not know what causes ADHD. There are no
specific lab tests, X rays, or scans that guarantee correct
diagnosis. However, we *do* know what ADHD looks like. We
know how it impinges on the lives of those who live around
these kids, teenagers, and adults who have it.

ADHD may be impacted by environmental factors or
dietary factors. (While I don't think dietary factors are big
contributors, they may make a small contribution to the disorder, so I'll talk more about that later.) There may be neurological factors. Poor parenting, teaching, or discipline may be
factors in some cases, causing a child to lack impulse control.

There may be an inherited tendency to develop ADHD
under certain circumstances. Russell A. Barkley, Ph.D., of
the University of Massachusetts Medical Center, estimates
that 40 percent of ADHD kids have at least one parent with
similar symptoms, and 35 percent have an affected sibling.[2]
If one identical twin is affected, the chances are between 80
percent and 92 percent that his or her sibling will be also.[3]

How common is ADHD? Is it overdiagnosed?
Some studies estimate that 1.7 percent of children have ADHD;
others claim the number is closer to 26 percent, depending
upon where, when, and how the studies were conducted.

The *Journal of the American Medical Association* (JAMA)
states that ADHD "is among the most common neurodevel-
opmental disorders in children."[4] The *British Medical Journal* estimates that some 7 percent of school-age children
have ADHD—and that boys are affected three times as often
as girls.[5] A 1995 Virginia study showed that 8 to 10 percent
of young school children were taking medication for ADHD.[6]

According to the Centers for Disease Control and Prevention (CDC) in 2002, 7 percent of children in the U.S. ages 6 to 11 had ADHD. They also reported that half of children in whom a diagnosis of ADHD was made also have a learning disability. They calculated that at least one million children have a learning disability without ADHD. The total number of children with at least one of these disorders was 2.6 million.[7]

Again, boys were three times as likely as girls to have a diagnosis of ADHD alone, and twice as likely to have ADHD with a learning disability. Rates of diagnosis of ADHD are twice as high in Caucasian children as in Latinos and African Americans. Interestingly, children with a diagnosis of a learning disability alone were more likely to live in a low income or single mother household, and children from families with health insurance were more likely to have a diagnosis of ADHD without a learning disability.[8]

It may be that Caucasian children, especially boys, are overdiagnosed. Another example is found in a study of fifth graders. Eighteen to 20 percent of Caucasian boys were being treated for ADHD with medication. African-American children with ADHD are less than half as likely to be receiving treatment.

Whether or not you believe ADHD is real, it is not at all uncommon. Those looking for help in dealing with ADHD are not alone. Many parents are trying to discover the attention deficit dividends of their child. There is hope. To unlock the potential in your child will require some work on your part, but it will be well worth it.

Undoubtedly, ADHD treatment is a controversial topic— but in my opinion it should not be. In fact, more and more the medical studies are confirming that treatments work and they help—and they should not be kept from children who need them.

I would be the first to admit that ADHD is occasionally overdiagnosed. Obviously, not everybody who is called ADHD really is. But overall, it appears that physicians and mental health professionals are doing a fair job. In fact, the *Journal of the American Medical Association* concludes: "Although some children are being diagnosed as having ADHD with insufficient evaluation and in some cases stimulant medication is prescribed when treatment alternatives exist, there is little evidence of widespread overdiagnosis or misdiagnosis of ADHD or of widespread overprescription of methylphenidate (Ritalin and others) by physicians."[9]

How can we tell if our child has ADHD instead of some other behavioral problem?

Indeed, there are many medical and mental health problems that can mimic some or many of the symptoms of ADHD. Likewise, completely normal children can, at various times in their development, share many of the traits or features seen in ADHD. That's why it's so important to have this condition diagnosed by a medical or mental health professional who is both trained and experienced in diagnosing and caring for ADHD. In my opinion, this needs to be someone who provides these services on a daily basis. Most primary care physicians (or even psychologists) don't do as good a job with this as our colleagues who provide this care as part of their everyday practice.

Although we don't have the space to review the conditions that can be confused with or co-exist with ADHD, here are just a few that an experienced health care giver will consider:

- Oppositional Defiant Disorder
- Pervasive Developmental Disorder
- Primary Disorder of Vigilance
- Central Auditory Processing Disorder
- Hearing problems
- Bipolar Disorder
- Anxiety disorders
- Tourette's Syndrome

- Fragile X Syndrome
- Vision disorders
- A wide variety of learning disorders
- Thyroid disorders
- Lead poisoning or toxicity
- Restless Leg Syndrome or other sleep disorders

Some people say ADHD is not a real disorder. What do you think?

Some so-called "experts" are trying to convince the lay public that ADHD is *not* real. ADD (Attention Deficit Disorder), now called ADHD (Attention Deficit Hyperactivity Disorder), is a real disorder. Frankly, I'd also like to avoid the term "disorder," preferring something like "Attention Deficit and Hyperactivity Dividends" or "Attention Deficit and Hyperactivity Differences." Those diagnosed with ADHD have a different brain structure and function. They approach life—work, play, and school—uniquely.

Don't be misled by those who try to convince you that ADHD is a diagnosis being foisted upon an unsuspecting public by psychiatrists and pharmaceutical companies so they can make money. Some believe this conspiracy theory, as discussed in *US News & World Report* in an article titled "Pushing pills on kids? Lawyers claim a conspiracy to oversell Ritalin."[10]

Yet in a well-publicized case involving the detractors and proponents of ADHD diagnosis, a group of physicians claimed it would make as much sense to throw out the diagnosis and proven treatments for ADHD as it would to do so for schizophrenia or epilepsy. Further, denying that ADHD is a real diagnosis of a real condition may be potentially dangerous to the people who live with it.

Nevertheless, criticism about the diagnosis and treatment of ADHD is repeated on Web sites, on the radio, in TV and magazine ads and stories—not to mention many popular books. One example is the book *Talking Back to Ritalin: What Doctors Aren't Telling You About Stimulants for Children.*[11] According to the author, Dr. Peter Breggin, national organizations that advocate ADHD, pharmaceutical companies, and even government institutes that fund ADHD research are conspiring to drug school children. Breggin, like many of the conspiracy theorists, never explained how this complex plan could be so well organized and remain so secret.

Russell A. Barkley, Ph.D., Director of Psychology and a Professor of Psychiatry and Neurology at University of Massachusetts Medical Center, concludes, "[Dr. Breggin's book] appears to be a carefully and cleverly crafted piece of artful propaganda against the diagnosis of ADHD and its treatment."[12] Worse yet, "Breggin's view must be taken for what it actually is—a not-so-subtle form of parent bashing that lays the blame for ADHD and other complex developmental and mental disorders at the feet of the child's parents, family and school."[13]

Barkley points out what parents of ADHD kids already know: Critics of ADHD "instruct parents to seek outdated, unscientific, and ineffective pop-psychological views of disorders and their treatment."[14]

Others have questioned whether ADHD is a "pathologic" disorder or merely one end of the continuum of age-appropriate behavior. For example, one psychologist writes:

> There seems to be a continuum of people all the way from those linear thinkers who are highly structured, intently focused, able to block out external stimuli, organized, and who even thrive on their attention to detail, to those analog thinkers who are hypersensitive to all stimuli, creative, always putting things together in new ways, and are more focused on the process or pattern of what is going on than the details involved in accomplishing the

tasks. These are the two extremes of the continuum, with most people falling somewhere in between.[15]

On the surface, the contention that ADHD is simply normal behavior seems somewhat reasonable. But to deny that ADHD exists flies in the face of an incredible volume of medical and psychological research. No doubt it's helpful to understand that your child is wired differently and that he or she will not fit well in the more linear or detail-oriented world. If we try to mold a child into someone he is not, not only can we harm his spirit, but we can also damage his self-esteem and block any chance he has of becoming the person he was created to be.

It has been helpful for my patients with ADHD kids (or who are ADHD themselves) to understand that the diagnosis and treatment of ADHD has more science and research backing it than the majority of the medical problems that occur in childhood. This research, along with an understanding of how to unlock your child's special potential and gifts, can help you as your child's "health care quarterback" choose the best health care providers and the best treatment options for ADHD to gain the dividends from your child's special and unique differences.

Bottom line? Parents with ADHD kids know it's real and they need help. Those of you who have a hyperactive, easily distractible youngster, you know that ADHD is a very real condition.

What are some of the traits seen in people with ADHD?
Hallowell and Ratey, authors of an excellent text titled *Driven to Distraction*, list 20 symptoms that are often evident in a person with ADHD.[16] They are:
1. A sense of underachievement, of not meeting one's goals (regardless of how much one has accomplished)

2. Difficulty getting organized
3. Chronic procrastination or trouble getting started
4. Many projects going simultaneously; trouble with follow-through
5. Tendency to say what comes to mind without necessarily considering the timing or appropriateness of the remark
6. An ongoing search for high stimulation
7. A tendency to be easily bored
8. Easy distractibility, trouble focusing attention, tendency to tune out or drift away in the middle of a page or a conversation, often coupled with an ability to focus at times
9. Often creative, intuitive, highly intelligent
10. Trouble going through established channels, following proper procedure
11. Impatient; low tolerance for frustration
12. Impulsive, either verbally or in action, as in impulsive spending of money, changing plans, enacting new schemes or career plans, and the like
13. Tendency to worry needlessly, endlessly; tendency to scan the horizon looking for something to worry about alternating with inattention to or disregard for actual dangers
14. Sense of impending doom, insecurity, alternating with high risk-taking
15. Depression, especially when disengaged from a project
16. Restlessness
17. Tendency toward active behavior
18. Chronic problems with self-esteem
19. Inaccurate self-observation
20. Family history of manic-depressive illness, depression, substance abuse, or other disorders of impulse control or mood

My daughter displays many of the symptoms of ADHD, but she isn't what I'd call hyperactive. What gives?

The *Diagnostic and Statistical Manual of Mental Disorders,* 4th edition (DSM-IV) identifies the three subtypes of ADHD as:

- ADHD: Predominately Hyperactive-Impulsive Type
- ADHD: Predominately Inattentive Type
- ADHD: Combined Type

The use of the word "hyperactivity" in the ADHD diagnosis can be misleading. Not all children with ADHD are constantly racing around, especially if they have Predominately Inattentive Type ADHD. The use of the term "attention deficit" can also be confusing. Boy and girls, men and women with ADHD, to the surprise of most, usually do not have a short attention span. Because of this, it is not at all unusual for them to become lost in something for long periods of time—especially if the activity is something that deeply interests them.

This interest can so occupy their concentration and attention that they are unaware of virtually anything going on around them. When you see this, what you are seeing is a manifestation of their almost unappeasable and inexorable need for mental stimulation and activity, a need that seems to last for virtually every moment they are awake.

Whether hyperactive or not, most ADHD children, adolescents and adults share one overriding characteristic—distractibility—and not just minor distractibility, but major, big-time, big-league distractibility.

My ADHD first grader is aggressive and easily frustrated at school. What's going on?

As these kids grow older, some react to too much or too little stimulation by "acting out" in the classroom or at day care. They may pull items off shelves, attack other kids, or seemingly "spin out of control" into a variety of silly behaviors. They can show signs of being hypersensitive to unusual sights or sounds. It is not unusual for these kids to have trouble adapting to changes in their daily routines and many (in one study, up to 63 percent[17]) demonstrate sleeping difficulties.

No doubt, most of these kids demonstrate very high levels of impulsive behavior, often at very early ages—even before the "terrible twos." Unusual behaviors for these youngsters can include erratic and aggressive actions such as hair pulling, biting, pinching or hitting others. Temper tantrums, normal in most children, are often exaggerated in ADHD children—not usually out of anger, but by over-stimulation or even affectionate behavior. I've seen many perplexed moms whose two or three year old has displayed aggressive and abrupt behavior when being cuddled or hugged.

Because of these patterns, studies now suggest that ADHD can usually be diagnosed by age four and should not be diagnosed in those whose symptoms appear after age seven.

Is ADHD associated with sugar intake?

Before we go any further, let's dispel a myth. Many of the parents of my childhood and teenage ADHD patients have strongly believed that sugar makes their kids hyper. One mom, speaking of her ADHD child, told me, "If my kid eats or drinks anything with sugar in it, he'll start bouncing off the walls. Yesterday, he had a snack that a friend gave him. For the next three hours, I couldn't calm him down."

Some of my patients even think that sugar causes ADHD. In fact, in a survey conducted by the University of Florida, 59 percent of African-American parents and 30 percent of Anglo parents attributed ADHD to excessive sugar in their kids' diets.[18] In another study, more than 80 percent of Canadian primary school teachers believed that sugar consumption contributed to increasing activity of normal children and to the behavioral problems of hyperactive children. Moreover, in the three years prior to the study, 55 percent of all teachers had counseled parents to consider reducing their child's sugar consumption to control hyperactivity, and parents frequently did so.[19] However, the available scientific evidence does not support the theory that sugar consumption has significant adverse effects on children's behaviors.[20]

In fact, in researching this chapter, I identified over 20 medical studies that have evaluated the effect of sugar on the behavior of children. In the majority of these studies kids were given food or drink containing either sugar or another sweetener such as saccharin or aspartame. Then the children were observed and/or tested for several hours. The studies were "blinded." In other words, neither the kids nor the researchers knew whether sugar or another sweetener had been ingested.

Here's an example of one of these studies: Researchers at Vanderbilt University conducted a double-blind controlled trial with two groups of children: 25 normal preschool children (3 to 5 years of age) and 23 school-age children (6 to 10 years) described by their parents as sensitive to sugar.[21] The children and their families followed a different diet for each of three consecutive three-week periods. One diet was high in sucrose with no artificial sweeteners, another was low in sucrose and contained aspartame as a sweetener, and the third was low in sucrose and contained saccharin (placebo) as a sweetener.

All the diets were essentially free of additives, artificial food coloring, and preservatives. The children's behavior and cognitive performance were evaluated weekly. The authors concluded, "Even when intake exceeds typical dietary levels, neither dietary sucrose nor aspartame affects children's behavior or cognitive function."[22]

Virtually all of the studies that I have reviewed have concluded that there is no difference in the behavior of the kids whether they are given sugar or not. In the very few studies in which an effect was noticed, it was very faint.

For example, in a study that tested kids' attention conducted at the Long Island Jewish Medical Center, children with ADHD who had been given sugar had slightly lower scores than the kids who had consumed aspartame.[23] But in a study at the University of Toronto, activity levels in children who had drunk sugar-sweetened Kool-Aid were slightly lower than those of children who had drunk aspartame-sweetened Kool-Aid.[24] These studies had the exact opposite results. However, in both of these studies the impact was barely perceptible. In fact, when doctors from Vanderbilt University looked at all 20 of these studies (in what is called a meta-analysis), they concluded that there was no evidence that sugar has any effect on a child's behavior or mental performance.[25] These authors concluded, "Sugar does not affect the behavior or cognitive performance of children. The strong belief of parents may be due to expectancy and common association."

But, despite the medical evidence, I find that most parents find it difficult to accept the findings that sugar does not change behavior. Why? Simply because many parents' observations are that when they give their kids sugar-containing food or snack drinks, they see their kids "go crazy"! Why is this? One explanation given by the experts is that the kids may be responding to some other ingredient in sweet foods or drinks, perhaps caffeine. This would be a possible culprit in soft drinks, as a can of cola can contain as much or more than the amount of caffeine in a cup of coffee.

Is ADHD caused by food additives?
Another possible cause of ADHD is reported to be food dyes or preservatives. For example, one study showed that up to 62 percent of children with ADHD had symptoms provoked by various food additives. But, the researchers now ask, is this a cause, or as in the case of sugar, is it an effect?

Dr. Ben Feingold first popularized the idea in his 1985

book, *Why Your Child Is Hyperactive*, that food additives caused ADHD.[26] However, multiple medical studies since then indicate that the likelihood of these substances playing a role in ADHD is very, very low. Although food dyes or preservatives may affect some children, it is at most a very small percentage *and* a very small effect.

The most likely explanation, once again, is *the parents'* expectations. Let me explain. If we believe that our children may react to sugar, dyes, or preservatives, then it is highly likely that we will see their activity as hyperactive—even when it is just normal activity. This was proven in a medical study at the Menninger Clinic.[27] They found a group of kids whose parents were convinced that they were reacting negatively to sugar. They then gave the kids Kool-Aid sweetened with aspartame and *not* sugar. The parents of half of the boys were told their sons had been given sugar. The other half was told that their boys had received a placebo drink with no sugar or aspartame.

The scientists then observed the parents interacting with their sons. Interestingly, the parents who had been told that their children had ingested sugar stayed much closer to their children and made more visible efforts to control their behavior. The researchers presumed that these parents were "expecting trouble."

The parents that were expecting the reaction also rated their boys' behavior as "hyperactive." This was true even though this group's activity levels were actually *lower*—that is, less active—than the boys whose parents had been told that their children had received a placebo drink.

You and I both know that our expectations can affect the way our children respond and behave. Furthermore, if we believe that sugar or additives make our kids act crazy and tell them this enough, they may well do what we predict!

The researchers also suggest another possibility—what they call "the special occasion effect." The effect occurs on those special family events, parties, or holidays when treats are liberally dispensed. These events can be especially exciting, or even stressful, for some children. Therefore, their behavior may simply be related to the event—not the sugar or additives.

Some kids are more likely to misbehave whenever their usual routine has been disrupted. This can look like hyperactivity, or may even *be* hyperactivity. But the cause is the disruption, not what they've eaten.

While it is highly unlikely that ADHD is either caused or worsened by junk foods, there are plenty of other health reasons to restrict these foods—at least on normal days.

How should I discipline my ADHD child?

One of our constituents wrote to Focus on the Family saying, "We have a five-year-old son who has been diagnosed with ADHD. He is really difficult to handle, and I have no idea how to manage him. I know he has a neurological problem; I don't feel right about making him obey like we do our other children. It is a big problem for us. What do you suggest?"

Dr. Dobson took the time to respond to this anguished mother, "I understand your dilemma, but I urge you to discipline your son. Every youngster needs the security of defined limits, and the ADHD boy or girl is no exception. Such a child should be held responsible for his or her behavior, although the approach may be a little different."

According to Dr. Dobson, "Most children can be required to sit on a chair for disciplinary reasons. However, the ADHD child would probably not be able to remain there. In the same way, spanking may actually be ineffective with some highly excitable children who are little bundles of electricity. As with every aspect of parenthood, disciplinary measures for the ADHD child must be suited to his or her unique characteristics and needs."[28]

What are some "Rules of Thumb" that you can use in training up these special gifts "in the way they should go"?

Here are 18 suggestions from a book by Dr. Domeena Renshaw titled *The Hyperactive Child.* Though her book is now out of print, Dr. Renshaw's advice is still valid:

1. Be consistent in rules and discipline.
2. Keep your own voice quiet and slow. Anger is normal. Anger can be controlled. Anger does not mean you do not love a child.
3. Try hard to keep your emotions cool by bracing for expected turmoil. Recognize and respond to any positive behavior, however small. If you search for good things, you will find a few.
4. Avoid a ceaselessly negative approach: "Stop"— "Don't"—"No."
5. Separate behavior, which you may not like, from the child's person, which you like, e.g., "I like you. I don't like your tracking mud through the house."
6. Have a very clear routine for this child. Construct a timetable for waking, eating, play, TV, study, chores, and bedtime. Follow it flexibly when he disrupts it. Slowly your structure will reassure him until he develops his own.
7. Demonstrate new or difficult tasks, using action accompanied by short, clear, quiet explanations. Repeat the demonstration until learned. This uses audiovisual-sensory perceptions to reinforce the learning. The memory traces of a hyperactive child take longer to form. Be patient and repeat.
8. Designate a separate room or a part of a room that is his own special area. Avoid brilliant colors or complex patterns in decor. Simplicity, solid colors, minimal clutter, and a worktable facing a blank wall away from distractions assist concentration. A hyperactive child cannot filter out overstimulation himself yet.
9. Do one thing at a time: Give him one toy from a closed box; clear the table of everything else when coloring;

turn off the radio/TV when he is doing homework. Multiple stimuli prevent his concentration from focusing on his primary task.

10. Give him responsibility, which is essential for growth. The task should be within his capacity, although the assignment may need much supervision. Acceptance and recognition of his efforts (even when imperfect) should not be forgotten.

11. Read his pre-explosive warning signals. Quietly intervene to avoid explosions by distracting him or discussing the conflict calmly. Removal from the battle zone to the sanctuary of his room for a few minutes is useful.

12. Restrict playmates to one or at most two at one time, because he is so excitable. Your home is more suitable, so you can provide structure and supervision. Explain your rules to the playmate and briefly tell the other parent your reasons.

13. Do not pity, tease, be frightened by, or overindulge this child. He has a special condition of the nervous system that is manageable.

14. Know the name and dose of his medication. Give it regularly. Watch and remember the effects to report back to your physician.

15. Openly discuss with your physician any fears you have about the use of medications.

16. Lock up all medications to avoid accidental misuse.

17. Always supervise the taking of medication, even if it is routine over a long period of years. Responsibility remains with the parents! One day's supply at a time can be put in a regular place and checked routinely as he becomes older and more self-reliant.

18. Share your successful "helps" with his teacher. The outlined ways to help your hyperactive child are as important to him as diet and insulin are to a diabetic child.[29]

Children with ADHD, however, have many other problems with which to deal. For example, compared to parents of children without ADHD, parents of kids with ADHD reported that their children were nearly three times more likely to have difficulty getting along with other kids in the neighborhood. Plus, the kids with ADHD were more than twice as likely to be picked on and less likely to have many good friends.

ADHD clearly also affects how children get along with friends and family, complete homework assignments and chores, and participate in after-school activities. Experts recommend a number of tips to help parents and children deal with the day-to-day problems that arise with living with ADHD:

- **Work with your child to create a plan.** Be aware of how ADHD can affect your child's life. Target each event—homework, fun, and family—then work with him or her to stay on track.
- **Maintain a regular schedule.** Work with your child to follow a consistent plan at home, in school, after school, and on weekends.
- **Build a support team that includes parents, teachers, instructors, youth pastors, and coaches.** Talk with them about how ADHD affects your child's life. Discuss successes and work together on the challenges.
- **Encourage participation in after-school activities.** Look for structured activities that use energy constructively and build social skills to bring success in and out of school.
- **Manage ADHD for the long-term.** Work with your doctor to develop a total treatment program, which may include long-acting medication that doesn't require frequent doses. To help your child stay focused all day, use techniques to help him modify his behavior.

- **Ease the strain of ADHD.** Keep routines fun and take breaks when times get tough to help relieve the stress of ADHD.
- **Recognize EVERY win.** Review your child's progress regularly and celebrate accomplishments, small and large.
- **Use available resources.** Take time to teach your child how to use calendars, organizers, and written reminders to help him or her stay focused all through the day.
- **Evaluate your child's personal strengths and weaknesses.** Managing ADHD requires discipline, a positive attitude, and good planning skills.
- **Understand the challenges of ADHD.** Know that ADHD is a medical problem that makes it more difficult to control behavior and attention.

What about Dad's involvement?

ADHD is much more commonly diagnosed in boys than in girls. When we look at the rash of shootings on school campuses today, boys are almost exclusively involved. When we look at campus violence, it's almost always the boys who are doing these things.

In his book *Bringing Up Boys*, Dr. James Dobson discusses the fact that many experts believe that one of the key causes of all this is the absence of fathers in the lives of their children—especially the boys. In the absence of paternal leadership and guidance, families are more likely to experience problems. Boys are made—created—to depend on their fathers, to listen to their fathers, to be molded by their fathers. That's the way God made them. You take men out of the lives of children, especially boys, and bad things usually happen.[30]

Some experts feel this phenomenon is even more crucial for the ADHD child. These boys and girls need their dads in their lives. For kids with impulse control problems, strong adult leadership—especially male leadership—appears to be crucial to model and teach that control.

For single moms with ADHD kids, getting one or more significant male role models in your kids' lives may be crucial. For the rest of you, Dad needs to be more involved. This will cost him time, no question about it. It may cost the family income or mean significant sacrifice and schedule change. But it will be an investment with magnificent returns. Quality time with kids, and especially ADHD kids, can only come inside of quantity time.

Options for Dealing with ADHD

A knowledgeable professional is needed to advise and encourage parents who are often bewildered and frustrated by behavior they can neither control nor understand. Finding a physician both trained and especially interested in caring for ADHD can be critical. In addition, there are numerous treatment options that can seem overwhelming when parents are trying to find help for their child. So, let's consider some medical and nonmedical interventions.

Diagnosing ADHD

The first step any good doctor is going to take is a comprehensive history of the problem. The most accurate diagnostic list is now felt to be the standardized checklist used in the DSM-IV. This is a diagnostic manual used by psychiatrists and other mental health professionals to guide their diagnosis of mental health conditions. In addition to the DSM-IV criteria, many physicians use standardized questionnaires for both the child's parents and teachers to fill out.

After the history, the physician should perform a complete physical exam to be sure that there are no other physical or neurological problems present.

Most physicians will order a basic set of blood and urine tests—once again, to rule out any medical problems that might mimic ADHD.

Although some physicians will use brain scans—such as a computerized tomography (CT) scan, a magnetic resonance image (MRI) scan, a single photon emission computed tomography (SPECT) scan, or a positron emission tomography (PET) scan—the only valid use for such an exam, outside of experimental protocols, is to make sure there are no other problems with the brain. In the future, such tests may be used in confirming a diagnosis of ADHD; however, the current state of the research does not allow for the routine use of these scans in the diagnosis of ADHD.

In the past, physicians (including myself) have used what we call "therapeutic trials" of prescription medications in the diagnosis of ADHD. Instead of doing a lot of expensive tests, we'd prescribe a stimulant medication, like Ritalin, and see if it helped or not. If the medication helped, that would (we thought) help make the diagnosis. However, this technique is no longer considered either valid or safe. For one reason, the stimulants can cause fairly severe side effects in kids who don't have ADHD. Second, a positive response to Ritalin can be seen in conditions other than ADHD. In this case, the falsely positive therapeutic trial would falsely label the child, prevent the child from getting a correct diagnosis, and cause him or her to take an unnecessary prescription. Third, as you are learning, ADHD treatment requires much more than just a prescription.

Diagnostic Criteria for ADHD

Most professionals who care for patients with ADHD use even more exact diagnostic criteria. In fact, these are the specific criteria for diagnosis from the DSM-IV:[1]

A. Either (1) or (2):

(1) Six (or more) of the following symptoms of inattention

have persisted for at least six months to a degree that is maladaptive and inconsistent with developmental level:

Inattention:

(a) Often fails to give close attention to details or makes careless mistakes in schoolwork, work, or other activities

(b) Often has difficulty sustaining attention in tasks or play activities

(c) Often does not seem to listen when spoken to directly

(d) Often does not follow through on instructions and fails to finish schoolwork, chores, or duties in the workplace (not due to oppositional behavior or failure to understand instructions)

(e) Often has difficulty organizing tasks and activities

(f) Often avoids, dislikes, or is reluctant to engage in tasks that require sustained mental effort (such as schoolwork or homework)

(g) Often loses things necessary for tasks or activities (for example, toys, school assignments, pencils, books, or tools)

(h) Is often easily distracted by extraneous stimuli

(i) Is often forgetful in daily activities

(2) Six (or more) of the following symptoms of hyperactivity-impulsivity have persisted for at least six months to a degree that is maladaptive and inconsistent with developmental level:

Hyperactivity:

(a) Often fidgets with hands or feet or squirms in seat

(b) Often leaves seat in classroom or in other situations in which remaining seated is expected

(c) Often runs about or climbs excessively in situations in which it is inappropriate (in adolescents or adults, may be limited to subjective feelings of restlessness)

    (d) Often has difficulty playing or engaging in leisure activities quietly

    (e) Is often "on the go" or often acts as if "driven by a motor"

    (f) Often talks excessively

   Impulsivity:

    (g) Often blurts out answers before questions have been completed

    (h) Often has difficulty awaiting turn

    (i) Often interrupts or intrudes on others (for example, butts into conversations or games)

B. Some hyperactive-impulsive or inattentive symptoms that caused impairment were present before age 7 years

C. Some impairment from the symptoms is present in two or more settings (for example, at school [or work] and at home)

D. There must be clear evidence of clinically significant impairment in social, academic, or occupational functioning

E. The symptoms do not occur exclusively during the course of pervasive developmental disorder, schizophrenia, or other psychotic disorder and are not better accounted for by another mental disorder (for example, mood disorder, anxiety disorder, dissociative disorder, or a personality disorder).

Although studies show that a mother's evaluation and description of these behaviors is very reliable and accurate, it is also clear that a mom or dad is unable to make the actual diagnosis. I want to emphasize that I list these criteria *not* so that you can make your own diagnosis. That is unsafe and inappropriate—especially in light of all of the medical and emotional problems that can mimic ADHD. But I do think seeing these criteria can be helpful to us as parents, especially if you feel your child is not getting a proper evaluation or treatment.

Parents should never be shy in advocating for their child's need. If your doctor is not as concerned about your child's behavior as you are (for example, if your child is an absolute angel in the doctor's office), then don't hesitate to insist upon a second opinion from an ADHD expert.

It is also important to point out that the criteria specifically indicate that the symptoms are "not due to oppositional behavior or failure to understand instructions." This is important to understand, as another common disorder in children and teens is the Oppositional-Defiant Disorder (ODD), which manifests itself with a pattern of persistent arguing with multiple adults, losing one's temper frequently, refusing to follow rules, blaming others, deliberately annoying others, and showing recurrent anger, resentfulness, spitefulness, and vindictiveness.

Dr. Bill Maier recently pointed out to me that between "40 and 60 percent of kids with ADHD may also have ODD. Many researchers believe that untreated ADHD can actually contribute to the development of ODD—a disorder which can wreak havoc on parents, teachers, and society."[2]

Nonmedication Treatments

There is no doubt that family counseling is helpful and educational for virtually every family wrestling with ADHD. Many parenting and communication skills can be learned and practiced. This therapy almost always helps the ADHD child, the parents, *and* the siblings learn ways to effectively communicate and cope during this potentially lifelong process of dealing with and managing ADHD. I would recommend this for all my ADHD families in my practice. Beyond family counseling, there are a number of psychological or psychiatric therapies (e.g., behavioral or cognitive therapies or biofeedback) that have been utilized with ADHD.

However, before beginning any therapy, be it behavioral or medication, the physician, parent, and patient should be very clear about the behaviors they are targeting for change—and those that are safe to leave alone. Since physicians have no way of predicting how any particular patient will respond to any particular therapy, all therapies for ADHD will involve a form of experimentation—a form of trial and error—to see what works and what does not. These trials will require your close observation and supervision. If one trial doesn't work, don't worry; there will be dozens of other options to consider.

Some ADHD experts use a purely behavioral strategy, and many parents can successfully help themselves and their ADHD children cope and succeed using behavioral principles and techniques alone. Further, some of these behavioral treatments have shown promise in early research.

There is certainly no harm in trying behavioral techniques prior to a trial of medication, and many of my patients have preferred such an approach. If you'd like to learn more, talk to a professional who is familiar with these approaches. But be aware that there are potentially harmful therapies to watch out for. For example, according to child psychologist Dr. Bill Maier, "One of the disturbing scams I'm aware of is the aggressive marketing being done by a large chain of biofeedback clinics. Their advertising uses scare tactics to prey on parents' fears about medication, and they charge huge fees for their treatment program. To my knowledge, there is no empirical validation that biofeedback therapy is effective in treating ADHD. Many parents are duped into spending their entire savings on this unproven treatment."[3]

Behavioral Therapies

A group of researchers has systematically reviewed the evidence for the effectiveness of a variety of behavioral therapies.[4] These authors looked at 58 studies that met their inclusion criteria. The results indicated that one specific form of behavioral therapy, cognitive behavioral treatment (CBT), does not improve the behavior or academic performance of children with ADHD. There are several different forms of CBT, but all emphasize the ability of people to make changes in their lives without having to understand why the change occurs.[5]

However, several specific psychological behavioral treatments that use the techniques and principles of behavior modification have consistently shown a benefit on behavior in medical studies. Beth Bruno explains, "The principles of behavior modification describe a formalized method that observes behavior and seeks to shape it in positive ways. The purposes of behavior modification in the education of children are *not* brainwashing, bribery or mind control. Quite the contrary. The purposes are to encourage children to experience the consequences of their actions in order to increase independence and self-discipline."[6] There are many different forms and types of behavior modification available.

Of great interest are the studies that look at the combined treatments consisting of a prescription drug and a behavioral intervention. One systematic review of the medical literature by Miller and his colleagues[7] looked at the effectiveness of combined treatments on ratings of behavior and identified three studies that met their inclusion criteria. The results, to my surprise, indicated that combined treatments did not differ significantly from medication alone. Jadad and his colleagues also reviewed the effectiveness of combination treatments. The results were similar to those obtained by Miller, as four of five studies showed little difference between combined treatments and stimulants alone. This does *not* mean that families dealing with ADHD should not obtain family counseling. Rather, it means that formal behavioral therapy may be no better than medication alone. Therefore, parents could, in good conscience, choose one option or the other.

But, whether you choose medication or behavioral therapy, a survey of more than 500 parents from the New York University Child Study Center[8] showed that children with ADHD may not be particularly compliant with either. The survey showed:

- Nearly 9 in 10 of these parents said that their children had been given medication to treat ADHD, but only about 50 percent of these kids were currently taking anything. The reasons? Nearly all these parents feared their children wouldn't receive the right dose of medicine at school and many said their children complained of side effects. Fortunately, we have a number of newer, longer-acting medications, which may dramatically reduce this particular problem.
- Nearly half of the parents who had children with ADHD said that behavior therapy had been recommended for their kids. But only 21 percent reported that their children actually participated in behavior therapy.

Furthermore, for children with the more severe forms of ADHD, there may be a significant risk of what the researchers call "school failure." One study followed a birth cohort of 1,265 children from an urban region of New Zealand until age 18 years.[9] Unfortunately, no formal diagnoses of attention deficit hyperactivity disorders were made, but the children were divided at age eight years into five groups with increasing attention difficulties, based on a behavioral rating scale. Children in the highest group of attention difficulties showed the highest proportion of school failures (60 percent) by age 18.

Caregivers Skills Program

Bose Ravenel, M.D., an emeritus member of the Physicians Resource Council at Focus on the Family and a practicing pediatrician for many years, explains a program that he is successfully using in his private practice:

Options for Dealing with ADHD

David Stein, Ph.D., the author of *Unraveling the ADD/ADHD Fiasco: Successful Parenting Without Drugs,* has described a novel behavioral approach to managing ADHD behaviors and reported encouraging data on [the] effectiveness of using this approach, without relying on stimulant medication.[10]

For those parents who might prefer to approach dealing with their child's ADHD behaviors without medication, Dr. Stein provides a conceptualization of ADHD and an approach that has been successful for some families. His Caregivers Skills Program (CSP) is based upon assumptions that depart from those upon which conventional behavioral management is based. These assume that ADHD children can be enabled and trained to develop those behavioral traits they lack, and that effective behavioral management relies upon avoiding material reinforcements, incentives, or token economy programs.

However, for CSP, no rules are posted, and contingency responses to target behaviors are imposed upon the slightest sign of inappropriate behavior. Accountability for appropriate behavior is transferred to the child. Reinforcement for appropriate behavior is stressed, consisting of social reinforcement only. The approach is considered strict, but not punitive.

The program depends entirely upon parental management of the target behaviors in the home environment and only involves the school in the small minority of cases where gains in the home environment do not generalize to the school. Stein's research has found that gains are realized whether behavioral problems are encountered primarily in the home or in school.

Stein found that 11 of 12 targeted ADHD behaviors improved dramatically or disappeared within four weeks among the 37 children fulfilling DSM-IV criteria for ADHD ages 5 to 11 years included in the study. These gains were stable at follow-up one year after treatment. In 81 percent of children, gains generalized to the school setting, and in the remaining 19 percent institution of a school component (daily report program) extended the behavioral improvement into the school setting.

Although the study is uncontrolled, the results appear to justify further clinical trials with control groups receiving alternative methods of management, considering the lack of evidence for long-term effectiveness of the prevailing medication centered approach and the virtual absence of risk.

Dr. Ravenel goes on to say:

The CSP approach is completely free of risk in contrast to the prevailing medication based approach. I have witnessed a number of cases of effective resolution of ADHD behaviors with the CSP approach in my general pediatric practice. I recognize that Stein's data are uncontrolled, and my case management success anecdotal, but the absence of risk of adverse effects suggests that trials of this revolutionary behavioral approach at least be done comparing results with conventional stimulant medication management.[11]

Nevertheless, there are potential problems with CSP that mean it may not be for everyone. Dr. Ravenel says, "I recognize that some parents will likely be unable or unwilling to devote the consistency of effort required for successful implementation of the CSP approach. Therefore, stimulant medication management will likely retain a place in management. Nevertheless, prudence suggests that its use be restricted to children or adolescents whose behaviors are more problematic and in circumstances where caretakers cannot or will not utilize the CSP approach successfully."

One of my favorite ADHD experts and researchers, Dr. Russell Barkley, at the University of Massachusetts Medical Center, seems to agree with Dr. Ravenel about the use of behavioral therapies in ADHD kids when he writes in the on-line version of *Scientific American*:

> Treatment for ADHD should include training parents and teachers in specific and more effective methods for managing the behavioral problems of children with the disorder. Such methods involve making the consequences of a child's actions more frequent and immediate and increasing the external use of prompts and cues about rules and time intervals. Parents and teachers must aid children with ADHD by anticipating events for them, breaking future tasks down into smaller and more immediate steps, and using artificial immediate rewards. All these steps serve to externalize time, rules, and consequences as a replacement for the weak internal forms of information, rules and motivation of children with ADHD.[12]

Although Dr. Stein and his CSP method actually advocate avoiding prompts and reminders and stimulants, Dr. Barkley feels strongly that behavioral approaches should be used "in addition to stimulant medications—and perhaps antidepressants, for some children."[13] Therefore, let's take a look at medications for ADHD.

Prescription Medications

Many, many parents call or write us at Focus on the Family to ask about using prescription medications for ADHD. They've heard the controversies and they are worried that starting a medication might be bad. On the other hand, many worry that not starting a medication may be harmful. They ask, "What should we do?"

Without a doubt, the use of prescription drugs for both

children and adults is one of the most successful short-term therapies available. There is a virtual mountain of evidence supporting the safety and effectiveness of using medications in ADHD, although these are all fairly short-term studies, with none going more than two years. According to these studies, anywhere from as few as 70 percent to as many as 95 percent of ADHD patients benefit from appropriate medication.[14] These medications seem to dramatically reduce disruptive behavior, improve school performance, and even raise IQ test scores. The medications seem to work equally well with boys and girls.

No one knows exactly how they work, but they probably affect the electrochemical processes in the brain, which regulate behavior. As noted above, they are *not* cure-alls, and, as noted below, they can have significant side effects. Further, they do not improve the ability to memorize and may not help language processing. In addition, they do not help social skills.

Prescription Stimulant Medications

The most commonly prescribed drugs are Ritalin, Concerta, Dexedrine, and Adderall. In most instances, these substances have a remarkably positive effect—at least for the short term.[15]

Yet parents are still rightly concerned about the overprescribing of these drugs. One parent wrote to my colleague, Dr. James Dobson, asking, "Do you worry about Ritalin and other drugs being overprescribed? Should I be reluctant to give them to my 10-year-old?" I thought his reply was timely and wise, "Prescription drugs have been used as a cure-all for various forms of misbehavior. That is unfortunate. We should never medicate kids just because their parents have failed to discipline them properly or because someone prefers to have them sedated. Every medication has undesirable side effects and should be administered only after careful evaluation and study."[16] I couldn't agree more.

What Is the Best Stimulant Option?

As I mentioned above, the treatment for ADHD should be individualized and tailored for each child and each family. So, while there is no "best" treatment, there are a number of excellent treatment options. Learning more about them can assist you in working with your child's physician to choose among these options.

One of the disturbing problems with using stimulant medications for ADHD has been the fact that the older medications didn't last very long. Their positive effects were not very long-lived—a few hours at most. This meant that extra doses would have to be given at school or later in the afternoon once the child was home. Worse yet, when the short-acting medications wore off, a "rebound effect" could occur where the child's symptoms and behaviors actually worsened! This not only created difficulty for the school, it also caused embarrassment for the child and led to noncompliance.

Other side effects with the stimulant medications include anxiety, nervousness, palpitations (rapid heart beat), sweating, and insomnia (difficulty going to sleep). More rare side effects include irritability, mood swings, depression, withdrawal, hallucinations, and "loss of spontaneity." The friends of one of my young patients told her, "Carla, please don't take your medication before you come to our party. You'll be no fun!"

But I have good news. Newer medications are now available to solve this problem for many patients.

I teach my patients that the stimulants that are used to treat ADHD can be thought of as short-, intermediate-, and long-acting. The short-acting tablets of methylphenidate (available in a generic form as well as in the brand names Ritalin and Methylin) and dextroamphetamine (available in a generic form as well as in the brand names Dextrostat and Dexedrine) have a quick onset of action, but they only last in the system for three to six hours—which is not long enough to get through the average school day.

Intermediate-acting medications such as Ritalin SR, Metadate ER, and Methylin ER have a much slower release into the system so their effects last longer—about six to eight hours. The regular form of a newer medication, called Adderall, also appears to last six to eight hours. This medication combines four kinds of stimulant medications. However, more than 50 percent of children require an additional dose later in the day. The newest medication in this group is Focalin (dexmethylphenidate, a new formulation of the most active portion of methylphenidate).

Recently, scientists have developed controlled-release systems that give the same effect as multiple daily doses of the short- or intermediate-release medications. These newer medications are called long-acting or once-daily preparations. They are specifically designed to help your child get through the entire day on a single dose.

Adderall XR uses intermediate- and delayed-release drug-containing beads to accomplish this. A 20-mg capsule of Adderall XR works the same as taking a 10-mg Adderall twice a day. And if your child cannot swallow a capsule, the contents can be sprinkled on a soft food such as applesauce.

Concerta (methylphenidate) works by using a specially patented system called the OROS delivery system. Some clinicians believe that Concerta has the longest duration of action, although this has not been formally studied yet.

Metadate CR acts through the use of intermediate- and extended-release beads. Some experts believe that the effects of Metadate CR are of shorter duration than Concerta. This may be an advantage for those on Concerta who have no appetite at suppertime or have trouble going to sleep from the prolonged effects of Concerta.

Dexedrine Spansules also contain beads and last 10-12 hours. Most of these products come in several different dosages, so they can be started at the lowest possible dose and then slowly increased.

These products release some of the drug immediately, so the effect is like giving a short-acting product. Then, they gradually release the drug over a period of hours so the effect is sustained throughout the day. For most children, this means no additional doses! However, the use of any of these drugs for ADHD is not inexpensive. Depending upon the medication and the prescribed dose, they can cost from $30 (for generic forms) to nearly $100 per month.

For a few children, symptoms may re-emerge in the late afternoon or early evening. For these kids, an intermediate-acting or short-acting preparation could be given in the early afternoon, right after school. However, this type of dosing does increase the chances that the child will have trouble going to sleep (insomnia).

The newest of the long-acting stimulants for ADHD is Ritalin LA. As of the writing of this book, it is undergoing FDA review. I expect it will be approved by the time you read this.

I should point out to you that these newer, long-acting products have not yet been compared to one another in head-to-head trials. So it may be worth trying an alternate product if one doesn't work. Also, they contain different drugs (methylphenidate, amphetamine salts, or dextroamphetamine). A particular child may respond to one but not to another.

Finally, there's one drug I cannot recommend. Pemoline (Cylert) has been used for decades for ADHD. However, the American Academy of Pediatrics and many other experts do *not* recommend Cylert for ADHD therapy, as it has been associated with fatal liver toxicity.[17] *The medicine is so poten-* ✗ *tially dangerous that many experts refuse to use it.*

Antidepressant Use in ADHD

For older adolescents and adults with ADHD, there's an increasing interest among medical professionals in using a

newer class of antidepressants called SSRIs when there is con-
current depression or anxiety. These Selective Serotonin Reuptake Inhibitors help regulate the neurotransmitter serotonin in
the brain. Some of the more common SSRIs that are used in
ADHD include fluoxetine (Prozac and Prozac Weekly), paroxe-
tine (Paxil and Paxil Weekly), and sertraline (Zoloft).

There are two newer drugs, called "designer antidepressants." Bupropion (Wellbutrin and Wellbutrin SR) and ven-
lafaxine (Effexor and Effexor XR) are now being used to treat
adults (and some adolescents) with ADHD and depression.
However, it may take several weeks to see a benefit.[18]

In one report, bupropion was shown to be effective in
treating adolescents with ADHD and conduct disorder problems. Some experts are even using bupropion for ADHD in
children.[19] These medications affect one or more of the
brain's neurotransmitters that are not targeted by other
antidepressants. And, many experts are starting to use these
antidepressants as first line drugs—even before trying stimulant medications.

Some physicians like to use the designer antidepressants
instead of the stimulants. They feel they have less potential
for abuse—by your kid's friends! In addition, they can be
used for adolescents or adults with ADHD and depression or
those who don't respond to stimulants.

One last class of antidepressants still used by some
physicians in the treatment of ADHD is the tricyclic antidepressants. This is an older class of medications that have
been available for decades. Examples include desipramine
(Norpramin) and imipramine (Tofranil, Tofranil-PM). In one
study of adults with ADHD, it was reported that desipramine
worked as well as Ritalin.

The tricyclics are much less expensive than the brand
name SSRIs or designer antidepressants. However, they may
have more side effects, including drowsiness and dry mouth.
Typically these side effects decrease over time. In addition,

case reports of sudden deaths in children taking tricyclics have caused concern. Although a rare side effect (and it is still questioned whether the tricyclic actually caused these deaths), most parents who are made aware of this possibility will choose other options.

In addition, case reports of delirium and tachycardia (a racing heart rate) in adolescents who take tricyclics and smoke marijuana cause some parents to choose other options for their teenagers.

Other Medication Options

Besides stimulants and antidepressants, there are several other medication options your physician may consider:

MAOI The monoamine oxidase inhibitor (MAOI) tranyl-cypromine (Parnate) has been reported to help some children with ADHD. However, taking it requires a significantly restricted diet and the avoidance of a number of over-the-counter drugs (including some common cough syrups, herbs, and supplements) and prescription drugs. In addition, fatal reactions have been reported when MAOIs and SSRIs have been taken together. Because of these interactions, most physicians use a MAOI only if no other options seem to work as well.

BuSpar The antianxiety drug buspirone (BuSpar) has been reported to help some children with ADHD and is currently being studied in children and adolescents with ADHD.

Catapres The alpha-2 antagonist clonidine (Catapres) is one of the most common "add-on" medications for ADHD. In other words, if a stimulant or antidepressant is not fully effective, many physicians will "add-on" clonidine as a second medication, especially for those children who have more problems with impulsivity and aggression.

This medication affects the neurotransmitter norepinephrine, an important chemical in the process of concentration. Uncommon side effects include dizziness, dry mouth, drowsiness, or constipation, which usually lessen over time. Also, clonidine can cause the heart to slow down and missing doses has been seen to cause tachycardia (rapid heartbeat) and other problems. A handful of deaths in children taking clonidine and Ritalin have been reported. Therefore, some experts recommend children be evaluated for heart or kidney problems.

Modafinil Approved only for the treatment of excessive daytime sleepiness associated with narcolepsy, Modafinil significantly improves the symptoms of ADHD in children, according to a study conducted by Dr. Joseph Biederman, professor of psychiatry at Harvard Medical School. Optimum dosing was not yet known at the time of this printing, yet it seems to be a good alternative for those patients who do not respond positively to stimulant therapies.[20]

Strattera (atomoxetine HCI) In January 2003, Strattera was released with FDA approval. In studies, the drug was shown to have fewer side effects than stimulants and controlled substances, and no risk of insomnia or addiction. It was the first new drug to be approved for ADHD in nearly three decades, and also the first nonschedule II drug. It can be indicated for the treatment of adolescents and adults and therefore may become first line therapy. At the time of this printing, clinical studies had yet to prove its effectiveness as opposed to stimulants, but as a selective norepinephrine reuptake inhibitor, researchers believe it has better ability to regulate norepinephrine than Catapres and with fewer side effects.[21]

Other medications Some physicians also use a drug similar to clonidine, guanfacine (Tenex). It causes less drowsiness than clonidine. A newer medication, tomoxetine, is also being studied in children with ADHD.

The anti-Parkinson's drug Sinemet (levodopa/carbidopa) has been given to kids with Restless Leg Syndrome (RLS). Kids with RLS and ADHD who have been treated with

Sinemet have been reported to show improvement in their ADHD. More research is currently being done on this medication in kids with ADHD.

Combined Medications

If a trial of an initial medication at one or more dosages or doses is not helpful, then the addition of a trial of a second or third medication is in order. However, some physicians will add a second medication early in the course of treatment and report that such additions are helpful. Whether it takes one or two medications, most physicians will aim to use the lowest effective dose. In addition, frequent follow-up with the physician is necessary to provide the best possible care.

Legitimate Concerns about Medications for ADHD

Parents, medical professionals, and the general population have expressed concerns about the widespread use of medication for ADHD. Indeed, these concerns are legitimate. According to a 1998 report from an expert panel convened by the National Institute of Mental Health, there are "many important questions regarding treatments [of ADHD] that remain unanswered."[22] Here are their concerns:

- No major studies have been published that have examined the long-term effects or effectiveness (more than two years) of either behavioral therapies or prescription medications.
- There are no national guidelines (or even reliable guidelines) on the treatment of the inattentive subtype of ADHD.
- There are no national guidelines for treating adolescents or adults with ADHD.
- There are no proven therapies for targeting some of the specific problems seen with ADHD, such as deficits in language processing or impaired working memory.

This is not to say that there are no therapies that can be applied to each of these situations and are being used successfully—at least based upon anecdotal reports. Nevertheless, more research is needed to conclusively answer these questions.

Evidence for the Use of Medications in ADHD

One group of researchers assessed the effectiveness of prescription stimulant drugs using a comprehensive systematic review of the many studies that have been published.[23] The authors identified 18 randomized controlled trials that used behavioral rating scales to measure the effect of stimulant medications. The review concluded that three drugs— methylphenidate (available as a generic and in the brands of Ritalin, Metadate ER, Methylin ER, Ritalin SR, Metadate CD, and Concerta), dextroamphetamine (available as a generic and in the brands of Dexedrine and Dexedrine Spansules), and pemoline (Cylert)—were all significantly more effective than placebo.

Studies have shown that some children who are unresponsive to or intolerant of methylphenidate have tolerated or responded well to dextroamphetamine, and vice versa. So, if one medication does not work, a trial of the other is usually considered appropriate.[24]

Another group of researchers looked at all the studies evaluating the effectiveness of the stimulants[25] and reported on 18 studies that compared stimulant drugs. In general, methylphenidate, dextroamphetamine, and pemoline were found to be equivalent.

These same researchers found nine studies that compared the effectiveness of tricyclic antidepressants with placebo: Five of six studies showed that desipramine (Norpramin) was more effective than a placebo. They also found one of three studies of imipramine (Tofranil, Tofranil-PM) reported a similar benefit to desipramine. Four studies compared stimulants with tricyclic antidepressants—sort of a head-to-head comparison. Unfortunately, the results were inconsistent.

One caveat about the stimulant medications: We simply have no long-term studies of either their safety or effectiveness. Countless people living with ADHD can attest to their safe and long-term use, but that anecdotal evidence is not nearly as helpful as actual research studies. One study, published in 1999, showed that taking stimulants for ADHD was both safe and effective for at least two years.[26] Other long-term studies are currently being performed.

Drug Vacations

When I was in my medical training at Duke, we were taught to try to give our ADHD patients drug holidays. The advice was to try to avoid medications on weekends, holidays, and vacation. Some physicians still ascribe to this practice; however, not only is there no evidence supporting this theory, there is evidence that this may, for some kids, be harmful. Why? Simply because those with ADHD, who are being successfully treated with medications, find that their social and family functioning is so improved on the medication that withholding it may actually contribute to peer rejection, family conflict, and reduced self-esteem.

Stimulant Medications and Drug Abuse

Some experts believe that children who take stimulant medications are at increased risk for drug abuse. There has been a lot of concern and debate about this over the years, causing some parents to shy away from using Ritalin or similar medications for ADHD.

Fortunately, this does not appear to be true. New research suggests that giving kids stimulants for ADHD does not increase their risk of illicit drug abuse later on.[27] Interestingly enough, it may be that just the opposite is true.

Children who are not treated for ADHD are more likely to abuse drugs than those who are treated. In fact, treating ADHD with prescription medications seems to reduce the risk of drug abuse by 84 percent.

If you think about it a bit, I bet this will make sense to you. Children with uncontrolled ADHD are more impulsive and likely to take risks, have lower self-esteem, and have fewer friends—all of which increase the chance they may experiment with alcohol or illicit drugs.

However, when it comes to tobacco use, one study has reported that kids with ADHD who were treated with stimulants had increased rates of daily smoking and tobacco dependence as compared with ADHD kids not treated with stimulants.[28]

Every medication has undesirable side effects and should be administered only when indicated and appropriate. Ritalin, for example, has a number of potential side effects. It can reduce the appetite and cause insomnia in some patients. Nevertheless, for the vast majority of ADHD patients, prescription treatments are remarkably effective and safe.

Dr. James Dobson assures parents, "If your child has been evaluated and diagnosed with ADHD by a professional who is experienced in treating this problem, you should not hesitate to accept a prescription for an appropriate medication. Some dramatic behavioral changes can occur when the proper substance is given to the proper child. A boy or girl who sits and stares off into the distance or one who frantically climbs the walls is desperately in need of help. To give that individual a focused mind and internal control is a blessing. Medication often provides that opportunity—sometimes for the very first time."[29]

One caution, however. The main danger of drug abuse from stimulants is from your child's friends or classmates who do *not* have ADHD and want to use the stimulant to "get high." In one study, 16 percent of ADHD children had been approached to sell, give, or trade their medication.[30] As bad as that is, the problem of Ritalin abuse seems to be worsening.

A January 2001 segment on NBC's "Dateline" reported widespread abuse of Ritalin among college students. A national survey showed that 2.8 percent of high school seniors in 1997 had used Ritalin at least once in the previous year without a physician's prescription.[31] These data agree with the testimony before Congress of the Drug Enforcement Administration (DEA) reporting that in 1999, 3 percent of high school seniors had used Ritalin without a doctor's prescription. Worse yet, there has been a tenfold increase in emergency room visits for abuse or use without a prescription of methylphenidate among children from 10 to 14 years old. The unauthorized use of Ritalin is now as likely as the use of cocaine.

So, to protect your ADHD child's friends, be sure to carefully supervise his or her use of stimulants.

Herbs and Other Alternative Therapies

Alternative treatments used for ADHD include neurofeedback, homeopathy, herbal medicines, iron supplements, and dietary modifications or supplements—and *many* others. One recent review of all of these therapies, and the evidence for and against them, was published in a respected alternative medicine journal.[32] These authors concluded, "Although anecdotal evidence is surfacing to support the efficacy of these alternatives, further research is needed before they can be regarded as effective, reliable treatments for ADHD. Therefore, the use of more conventional treatments should be considered if alternative interventions prove unsuccessful."

Neurofeedback is one of the more interesting experimental therapies for ADHD. This technique uses electronic machines to teach kids with ADHD to slow down or speed up their brain waves—electronic signals in the brain. In one study neurofeedback was used in kids who attended four 50-minute sessions (twice a week for two weeks). In this small study, Ritalin use dropped from 30 percent to 6 percent.[33] The parents reported improvements in inattention, impulsivity, and concentration. More surprising was an average 12-point jump in the kids' IQs. Other studies have also shown positive effects.[34] Controlled studies are now testing this technique.

Natural therapies have virtually no research to tell us if they are safe or effective. Nevertheless, they are increasingly being promoted for ADHD—via TV and radio infomercials and on the Internet. Just a few include products like Efalex Focus, Pedi-Active, Kid's Companion Attention/Memory Formula, and many, many others.[35]

It's not uncommon to see manufacturers creating a wide variety of formulas based upon either animal research or extremely preliminary and limited human research. Then, they often will make big leaps to claim clinical effectiveness. Here are just a few examples that you might come across:[36]

Essential fatty acids (EFAs), such as gamma-linolenic acid (GLA) and docosahexaenoic acid (DHA), are sometimes low in kids with ADHD . . . but so far, there's no convincing evidence that replacing these nutrients helps.

Phosphatidylserine, a biologically active chemical commonly called PS, is normally found in the central nervous system (CNS)—the brain, spinal cord, and nerves. PS has been shown to improve cognitive function in Alzheimer's patients . . . but the effectiveness of PS in ADHD has not been proven.

Acetyl-carnitine is used to increase the neurotransmitter acetylcholine in the CNS. It can improve memory in elderly patients with dementia . . . but there's no proof that it's beneficial for ADHD.

DMAE (dimethylaminoethanol), also called deanol, is a

precursor to acetylcholine. It was marketed years ago as a prescription medication for ADHD called Deaner, but it was discontinued because it didn't work very well. As for deanol, which is still available, the *Natural Medicines Comprehensive Database* says, "Clinical studies using deanol for treating attention deficit disorder have produced inconclusive results."

Ginkgo biloba is a natural medicine that is commonly used to enhance cognitive function, but there's no reliable evidence that it will help patients with ADHD and no evidence that it is safe in children.

Ephedra (also called Ma huang) has stimulant effects, but it's not necessarily safe or effective for treating ADHD. Increasing reports of fatalities and severe side effects of this herb are leading more and more experts to condemn its use—especially in children. The *Natural Database* says that the use of Ephedra is "possibly unsafe when used orally. There is concern that use of ephedra can cause severe life-threatening or disabling adverse effects in some people." As for its use in children, the *Database* says, "Children can be more susceptible to the adverse effects of ephedra."

In fact, experts are now warning against giving most herbs or supplements to children because of potential side effects. Further, most herbs and supplements have never been tested in children or teenagers. One expert source says, "Steer parents away from these unproven treatments. Remind them that 'natural' doesn't necessarily mean safe."[37]

Natural Medicines Comprehensive Database (NMCD)

Because so much of the advertising about natural medicines (herbs, vitamins, and supplements) is false or misleading and because labeling of these products in the U. S. can be false or deceptive, it is valuable to have an accurate, evidence-based, and trustworthy source for information about these substances.

In my opinion, the NMCD is just that. It is very expensive and usually requires a subscription to access. However, readers of this book can access this database for no charge. Just go to our Focus on Your Family's Health Web site and click on the NMCD icon.

Can I Use Medications Only?

The proper care for people with ADHD *never* involves *just* medication. There are many aspects of living with ADHD that simply *cannot* be treated with a medication. Nevertheless, in seeking the optimal approach to treating ADHD, medication may play an extremely important role—but it's not the only answer.

On the other hand, as we've discussed, stimulant medications definitely work for the majority of ADHD cases. In most cases, it is not a question of whether the medication works—it works extremely well for most children who have this condition. Nevertheless, medications should be seen only as a tool that helps the child's caregivers implement behavior management, parenting, and teaching strategies that help this child come to more maturity.

Appendix I
American Academy
of Pediatrics Guidelines

The American Academy of Pediatrics (AAP) has now released national guidelines on the diagnosis, evaluation, treatment, and management of ADHD.[1] They recommend that parents have the diagnosis of ADHD confirmed by a professional using specific (e.g. DSM-IV) diagnostic criteria *and* a parent and teachers' rating scale such as the Conner's Scale.

They recommend that you be sure your child's doctor evaluates your child for the potential risk of additional psychiatric disorders. Then, after the diagnosis has been made, they recommend that you consider the risks, benefits, and costs of either behavioral or medication therapy.

The AAP recommends that you be sure that your child is scheduled for frequent follow-up evaluations with your child's doctor, as ADHD can be chronic and requires a long-term approach to management.

They remind us that treatment approaches and regimens almost always will need to be adjusted over time, as your child grows and as her social situation changes—such as changes in school, teachers, or classrooms.

Finally, they conclude that we should be sure to use a teamwork approach to care that includes the child and teachers, pastors, coaches, and other significant people.

The AAP guidelines for the diagnosis and evaluation of ADHD, as well as the treatment options and goals, are available for professionals and parents (www.aap.org/policy/ac0002.html) (www.aap.org/policy/s0120.html). A downloadable handout for parents which summarizes these technical papers and guidelines is also available at the Web site (www.aap.org/policy/ADHD.pdf).

Appendix II
Resource Groups

Here are a few resource groups you can count on for timely, accurate, and reliable information.

CHADD—Children and Adults with Attention-Deficit/Hyperactivity Disorder

8181 Professional Place, Suite 201, Landover, MD 20785
800-233-4050 or 301-306-7070
www.chadd.org

A non-profit, national, parent-based organization that provides support and disseminates information on attention deficit disorders to children and adults with ADHD. CHADD has over 32,000 members and more than 500 chapters nationwide.

Publications: *ATTENTION!* (Quarterly magazine); *CHADDER* (quarterly newsletter).

Attention Deficit Disorder Association

1788 Second St., Suite 200
Highland Park, IL 60035
847-432-ADDA
www.add.org

The Attention Deficit Disorder Association (ADDA) is a non-profit organization comprised of ADHD support group leaders, parents of ADHD children, and adults with ADHD. ADDA lends its experience to providing educational tools and resources, and advocating on behalf of those afflicted by ADHD and their families.

National Institute of Mental Health, National Institutes of Health
6001 Executive Blvd., Rm 8184, MSC 9663
Bethesda, MD 20892
301-443-4513
www.nimh.nih.gov (hit the "search" button, enter "ADHD", and then hit "enter")

The National Institute of Mental Health (NIMH), a component of the National Institutes of Health (NIH), conducts and supports research that seeks to understand, treat, and prevent mental illness. Information on NIMH-sponsored meetings, workshops, and symposia is available on the Institute's Web site.

National Mental Health Association
2001 N. Beauregard St., 12th Floor
Alexandria, VA 22311
800-969-6642
www.nmha.org/ (hit the "search" button, enter "ADHD", and then hit "enter")

The National Mental Health Association (NMHA) has national, state, and local chapters that provide information and support.

A publications catalog is available on request. Serial publication: *The Bill* (monthly newsletter)—news of conferences and workshops, current mental health legislation, and media activities.

National Information Center for Children and Youth with Disabilities
P.O. Box 1492, Washington, DC 20013-1492
800-695-0285
www.nichcy.org

This organization provides information on the educational and legal rights that you have—state by state. It also has excellent parent guides for ADHD and learning disabilities.

A.D.D. Warehouse
300 Northwest 70th Avenue, Suite 102, Plantation, FL 33317
800-233-9273
www.addwarehouse.com
    An excellent supplier of ADHD information and educational resources.

Online Newsletter by David Rabiner, Ph.D.
www.HelpforADD.com
    Updates on all the recent studies pertinent to ADHD. Solid and sensible.

Notes

Note: Notes marked with an asterisk (*) indicate informa-
tion obtained from the National Center for Biotechnology
Information Web site, PubMed (service of the National
Library of Medicine, National Institute of Health).
(www.ncbi.nlm.nih.gov/entrez/query.fcgi?db=PubMed)

Chapter One

1. Edward Hallowell, M.D. and John Ratey, M.D., *Driven to Distraction: Recognizing and Coping With Attention Deficit Disorder from Childhood through Adulthood* (New York: Simon & Schuster, 1995).

Chapter Two

1. Bonnie Cramond, Ph.D., "Attention Deficit Hyperactivity Disorder and creativity—What is the connection?" *Journal of Creative Behavior,* 28, no. 3 (1994): 193.
2. Les Linet, M.D., "The Search for Stimulation: Understanding Attention Deficit / Hyperactivity Disorder," *Healthology Press,* February 2002 (www.abcnews.go.com/sections/living/Healthology/und erstand_adhd020221.html).

Chapter Three

1. Thom Hartmann, Janie Bowman, Susan Burgess, eds., *Think Fast! The ADD Experience* (Grass Valley, Calif.: Underwood Books, 1996).
2. R. J. DeGrandpre, *Ritalin Nation: Rapid-Fire Culture and the Transformation of Human Consciousness* (New York: W.W. Norton & Company, 2000).

3. D. Papolos, M.D., and J. Papolos, *The Bipolar Child* (New York: Broadway Books, 1999), data taken from Chapter 6.
4. Dr. James C. Dobson, *Solid Answers* (Wheaton, Ill.: Tyndale House Publishers, Inc., 1997), p.68.

Chapter Four

1. Martha Denckla, M.D., Director of the Department of Developmental Cognitive Neurology at the Kennedy-Drieger Institute at Johns Hopkins.
2. J. J. Gillis, J. W. Gilger, B. F. Pennington, J. C. DeFries, "Attention deficit disorder in reading-disabled twins: evidence for a genetic etiology," *Journal of Abnormal Child Psychology,* June 1992, pp. 303-15.*
3. H. Gjone, J. Stevenson, J. M. Sundet, "Genetic influence on parent-reported attention-related problems in a Norwegian general population twin sample," *Journal of the American Academy of Child and Adolescent Psychiatry,* May 1996, pp. 588-96.*

Chapter Five

1. Jeffrey Freed and Laurie Parsons, *Right-Brained Children in a Left-Brained World* (New York: Simon & Schuster/Fireside, 1997), p. 233.
2. Gary Mihoces, "Amputations don't pin down wrestler," May 28, 2001 (www.usatoday.com/sports/ncaa/2001-03-28-wrestling.htm).
3. N. M. Lambert, C. S. Hartsough, "Prospective study of tobacco smoking and substance dependence among samples of ADHD and non-ADHD participants," *Journal of Learning Disabilities,* November-December 1998, pp. 533-44.*
4. J. Biederman, T. Wilens, E. Mick, T. Spencer, S. V.

Faraone, "Pharmacotherapy of attention-deficit/hyper-activity disorder reduces risk for substance use disorder," *Pediatrics,* August 1999, p. e20.*

5. Marc Eliot, *Walt Disney: Hollywood's Dark Prince* (New York: Birch Lane Press, Carol Publishing, 1993), pp. 200-201.

6. Dr. James C. Dobson, *ADD/ADHD: Facts and Encouragement* (Part 1), booklet. (Colorado Springs: Focus on the Family, 1990).

7. Ibid.

8. H. Bloch, "Life in Overdrive," *Time,* July 18, 1994, p. 48.

9. Dobson, *Facts and Encouragement.*

10. Bloch, p. 44.

11. Dobson, *Facts and Encouragement.*

12. Betsy Morris, "Overcoming Dyslexia," *Fortune,* May 13, 2002, p. 58.

13. Ibid., p. 66.

Chapter Six

1. Morris, "Overcoming Dyslexia," p. 56.

Chapter Seven

1. Ned Owens, M.Ed.

Chapter Nine

1. Sari Solden, *Women with Attention Deficit Disorder* (Grass Valley, Calif.: Underwood, 1995).

Chapter Ten

1. Dr. Kathleen Nadeau, on "ABC News."

2. J. Elia, P. Ambrosini, J. Rapoport, "Treatment of attention-deficit-hyperactivity disorder," *New England Journal of Medicine,* March 1999, pp. 780-88.*

3. B. Booth, W. Fellman, J. Greenbaum, et al., "Myths about ADD/ADHD," www.add.org/content/abc/myths.htm.

Chapter Eleven
1. Paul Elliott, M.D.
2. R. A. Barkley, "Genetics of childhood disorders: XVII. ADHD, Part 1: The executive functions and ADHD," *JAACAP,* August 2000, pp. 1064-68.*
3. Ibid.
4. L. Goldman, M. Genel, R. Bezman, P. Slanetz, "Diagnosis and treatment of attention-deficit/hyperactivity disorder in children and adolescents," *Journal of the American Medical Association,* April 1998, pp. 1100-1107.*
5. J. P. Guevara, M. T. Stein, "Evidence based management of attention deficit hyperactivity disorder," *British Medical Journal,* November 2001, pp. 1232-35.*
6. G. B. LeFever, K. V. Dawson, A. L. Morrow, "The extent of drug therapy for attention deficit-hyperactivity disorder among children in public schools," *American Journal of Public Health,* September 1999, pp. 1359-64.*
7. Centers for Disease Control and Prevention report, May 2002 (www.cdc.gov/nchs/releases/02news/attendefic.htm).
8. Ibid.
9. Goldman, et al., "Diagnosis and treatment of attention-deficit/hyperactivity disorder in children and adolescents," *JAMA,* pp. 1100-1107.*
10. Nancy Shute, "Pushing pills on kids? Lawyers claim a conspiracy to oversell Ritalin," *US News & World Report,* October 2, 2000, p. 60 (www.usnews.com).

11. Peter Breggin, *Talking Back to Ritalin: What Doctors Aren't Telling You About Stimulants for Children* (Common Courage Press: Monroe, Md., 1998).
12. R. A. Barkley, "ADHD, Ritalin, and Conspiracies: Talking Back to Peter Breggin," 1998 (www.quackwatch.org/04ConsumerEducation/NegativeBR/breggin.html).
13. Ibid.
14. Ibid.
15. Ibid.
16. Hallowell and Ratey, *Driven to Distraction*, pp. 73-76.
17. R. D. Chervin, K. H. Archbold, J. E. Dillon, P. Panahi, K. J. Pituch, R. E. Dahl, C. Guilleminault, "Inattention, hyperactivity, and symptoms of sleep-disordered breathing," *Pediatrics,* March 2002, pp. 449-56.*
18. J. R. Prinz, W. A. Roberts, E. Hantman, "Dietary correlates of hyperactive behavior in children," *Journal of Consulting and Clinical Psychology,* December 1980, pp. 760-69.*
19. D. DiBattista, M. Shepherd, "Primary school teachers' beliefs and advice to parents concerning sugar consumption and activity in children," *Psychological Reports,* February 1993, pp. 47-55.*
20. Ibid.
21. M. L. Wolraich, S. D. Lindgren, P. J. Stumbo, L. D. Stegink, M. I. Appelbaum, M. C. Kiritsy, "Effects of diets high in sucrose or aspartame on the behavior and cognitive performance of children," *NEJM,* June 1994, pp. 1902-3.*
22. Ibid.
23. E. H. Wender, M. V. Solanto, "Effects of sugar on aggressive and inattentive behavior in children with attention deficit disorder with hyperactivity and normal children," *Pediatrics,* November 1991, pp. 960-66.*

Notes

24. L. A. Rosen, S. R. Booth, M. E. Bender, M. L. McGrath, S. Sorrell, R. S. Drabman, "Effects of sugar (sucrose) on children's behavior," *JCCP,* August 1988, pp. 583-89.*
25. M. L. Wolraich, D. B. Wilson, J. W. White, "The effect of sugar on behavior or cognition in children. A meta-analysis," *JAMA,* November 1995, pp. 1617-21.*
26. B. F. Feingold, *Why Your Child Is Hyperactive* (New York: Random House, 1985).
27. D. W. Hoover, R. Milich, "Effects of sugar ingestion expectancies on mother-child interactions," *Journal of Abnormal Child Psychology,* August 1994, pp. 501-15.*
28. Dobson, *Facts and Encouragement* (Part 2).
29. D. Renshaw, *The Hyperactive Child* (Chicago: Nelson-Hall Publishers, 1974), pp. 118-20.
30. Dr. James Dobson, *Bringing Up Boys* (Wheaton, Ill.: Tyndale House Publishers, 2002), chapter 5.

Chapter Twelve

1. Reprinted with permission from *Diagnostic and Statistical Manual of Mental Disorders,* Fourth Edition (Washington, DC: American Psychiatric Association, 1994).
2. From personal communication, 2002.
3. Ibid.
4. W. Pelham, T. Wheeler, A. Chronis, "Empirically supported psychosocial treatments for attention deficit hyperactivity disorder," *JCCP,* June 1998, pp. 190-205.*
5. Raymond Lloyd Richmond, Ph.D., "Types of Psychological Treatment," from the Web site "A Guide to Psychology and its Practice": (www.guidetopsychology.com/txtypes.htm).
6. Beth Bruno, "Issues in Education: Behavioral Modification," *SNET Internet* Web site (www.snet.net/features/issues/articles/1998/05150101.shtml).

7. A. Klassen, A. Miller, P. Raina, S. K. Lee, L. Olsen, "Attention-deficit hyperactivity disorder in children and youth: a quantitative systematic review of the efficacy of different management strategies," *Canadian Journal of Psychiatry,* December 1999, pp. 1007-16.*
8. R. T. Brown, K. A. Borden, M. E. Wynne, A. L. Spunt, S. R. Clingerman, "Compliance with pharmacological and cognitive treatments for Attention Deficit Disorder," *JAACAP,* July 1987, pp. 521-26.*
9. D. M. Fergusson, L. J. Horwood, "The Christchurch Health and Development Study: review of findings on child and adolescent mental health," *The Australian and New Zealand Journal of Psychiatry,* June 2001, pp. 287-96.*
10. Dr. David B. Stein, "A medication-free parent management program for children diagnosed as ADHD," *Ethical Human Sciences and Services* (Journal, published by Center for the Study of Psychiatry and Psychology), 1999, pp. 61-79.
11. Dr. David B. Stein, *Unraveling the ADD/ADHD Fiasco* (Kansas City: Andrews McMeel, 2001). Data taken from chapter three.
12. Russell A. Barkley, *Attention-Deficit Hyperactivity Disorder* (New York: Guilford Press, 1998).
13. Ibid.
14. S. Pliszka, "The Use of Psychostimulants in the Pediatric Patient," *Pediatric Clinics of North America,* October 1998, p. 1087, citing J. Elia, B. G. Borcherding, J. L. Rapoport, C. S. Keysor, "Methylphenidate and dextroamphetamine treatments of hyperactivity: are there true nonresponders?" *Psychiatry Research* February 1991, pp. 141-55.*
15. "Medication for children with attentional disorders." American Academy of Pediatrics Committee on

Children With Disabilities and Committee on Drugs, *Pediatrics,* August 1996, pp. 301-4.*

16. Dobson, *Facts and Encouragement* (Part 2).
17. AAP, Subcommittee on ADHD, "Clinical practice guideline: treatment of the school-aged child with attention-deficit/hyperactivity disorder," *Pediatrics* 2001, pp. 1033-44.*
18. C. K. Conners, C. D. Casat, C. T. Gualtieri, E. Weller, M. Reader, A. Reiss, R. A. Weller, M. Khayrallah, J. Ascher, "Bupropion hydrochloride in attention deficit disorder with hyperactivity," *JAACAP,* October 1996, pp. 1314-21.*
19. Ibid.
20. Jill Stein, "Modafinil may have a role in the treatment of ADHD in children," 10-29-2002, Reuters Health (www.reutershealth.com).
21. "FDA approval of new ADHD drug opens options," 11-28-2002, Reuters Health.
22. "Diagnosis and Treatment of Attention Deficit Hyperactivity Disorder," National Institutes of Health (NIH) Consensus Statement, November 1998 (http://consensus.nih.gov/cons/110/110_statement.htm).
23. A. Klassen, et al., "Attention-deficit hyperactivity disorder in children and youth: a quantitative systematic review of the efficacy of different management strategies," *CJP,* pp. 1007-16.*
24. J. Elia, et al., "Methylphenidate and dextroamphetamine treatments of hyperactivity: are there true nonresponders?" *PR,* pp. 141-55.*
25. A. Jadad, M. Boyle, C. Cunningham, M. Kim, R. Shachar, "The treatment of attention-deficit/hyperactivity disorder," Evidence report/technology assessment (Summary), November 1999, pp. 1-341.*
26. "A 14-month randomized clinical trial of treatment strategies for attention-deficit/hyperactivity disorder,"

Notes

The MTA Cooperative Group. Multimodal Treatment Study of Children with ADHD. *Archive of General Psychiatry,* December 1999, pp. 1073-86.*

27. J. Biederman, et al., "Pharmacotherapy of attention-deficit/hyperactivity disorder reduces risk for substance use disorder," *Pediatrics,* p. e20, and S. Y. Hill, J. Locke, L. Lowers, J. Connolly, "Psychopathology and achievement in children at high risk for developing alcoholism," *JAACAP,* July 1999, pp. 883-91.*

28. N. M. Lambert, C. S. Hartsough, "Prospective study of tobacco smoking and substance dependence among samples of ADHD and non-ADHD participants," *Journal of Learning Disabilities,* November–December 1998, pp. 533-44.*

29. Dobson, *Facts and Encouragement* (Part 2).

30. C. J. Musser, P. A. Ahmann, F. W. Theyer, P. Mundt, S. K. Broste, N. Mueller-Rizner, "Stimulant use and the potential for abuse in Wisconsin as reported by school administrators and longitudinally followed children," *Journal of Developmental Behavior Pediatrics,* June 1998, pp. 187-92.*

31. C. Sannerud, G. Feussner, "Is Ritalin an abused drug? Does it meet the criteria of a schedule II substance?" in: Laurence L. Greenhill, Betty B. Osman eds., *Ritalin: Theory and Practice, 2nd ed.* (New York: Mary Ann Liebert, Inc., 2000), p. 37.

32. A. W. Brue, T. D. Oakland, "Alternative treatments for attention-deficit/hyperactivity disorder: does evidence support their use?" *Alternative Therapies in Health and Medicine,* January–February 2002, pp. 68-70, 72-74.*

33. L. Thompson, M. Thompson, "Neurofeedback combined with training in metacognitive strategies: effectiveness in students with ADD," *Applied Psychophysiology and Biofeedback,* December 1998, pp. 243-63.*

34. J. F. Lubar, M. O. Swartwood, J. N. Swartwood, P. H. O'Donnell, "Evaluation of the effectiveness of EEG neurofeedback training for ADHD in a clinical setting as measured by changes in T.O.V.A. scores, behavioral ratings, and WISC-R performance," *Biofeedback and Self-Regulation,* March 1995, pp. 83-99, and M. Linden, T. Habib, V. Radojevic, "A controlled study of the effects of EEG biofeedback on cognition and behavior of children with attention deficit disorder and learning disabilities," *Biofeedback and Self-Regulation,* March 1996, pp. 35-49.*

35. "Prescriber's Letter," Volume 7, September 2000. A service of Therapeutic Research Faculty (www.prescribersletter.com).

36. J. M. Jellin, F. Batz, K. Hichens, eds., *Natural Medicines Comprehensive Database, 3rd Edition* (Stockton, Calif.: Therapeutic Research Faculty, 2000) (www.naturaldatabase.com).

37. *Alternative Medicine: The Christian Handbook* is endorsed by the Christian Medical Association and is available from Focus on the Family. It contains the evidence supporting the 50 most commonly used alternative therapies in America (everything from acupuncture to yoga), and the 100 most commonly purchased herbs, vitamins, and supplements (everything from aloe to zinc).

Appendix I

1. AAP, Subcommittee on ADHD, "Clinical practice guideline: Evaluation and Diagnosis of the School-Aged Child with Attention-Deficit/Hyperactivity Disorder," *Pediatrics,* October 2001, pp. 1033-44.*

FOCUS ON THE FAMILY®

$\mathcal{W}$elcome to the $\mathcal{F}$amily!

Whether you received this book as a gift, borrowed it, or purchased it yourself, we're glad you read it. It's just one of the many helpful, insightful, and encouraging resources produced by Focus on the Family.

In fact, that's what Focus on the Family is all about—providing inspiration, information, and biblically based advice to people in all stages of life.

It began in 1977 with the vision of one man, Dr. James Dobson, a licensed psychologist and author of 18 best-selling books on marriage, parenting, and family. Alarmed by the societal, political, and economic pressures that were threatening the existence of the American family, Dr. Dobson founded Focus on the Family with one employee and a once-a-week radio broadcast aired on only 36 stations.

Now an international organization, the ministry is dedicated to preserving Judeo-Christian values and strengthening and encouraging families through the life-changing message of Jesus Christ. Focus ministries reach families worldwide through 10 separate radio broadcasts, two television news inserts, 13 publications, 18 Web sites, and a steady series of books and award-winning films and videos for people of all ages and interests.

• • •

For more information about the ministry, or if we can be of help to your family, simply write to Focus on the Family, Colorado Springs, CO 80995 or call 1-800-A-FAMILY (1-800-232-6459). Friends in Canada may write Focus on the family, P.O. Box 9800, Stn. Terminal, Vancouver, B.C. V6B 4G3 or call 1-800-661-9800. Visit our Web site—www.family.org—to learn more about Focus on the Family or to find out if there is an associate office in your country.

We'd love to hear from you!

Encouragement for Parents From Focus on the Family ®

The Mom You're Meant to Be

Motherhood is meant to be a blessing, not a burden. So why do so many moms seem exhausted and frustrated? Cheri Fuller encourages moms to relax, embrace their children's individuality and rely on God for the wisdom they need. Through engaging stories from her own days as a mother of young children, Cheri reassures moms to enjoy the experience of motherhood without worrying about finding the right "formula" to follow. Hardcover.

Creative Correction

You may recognize her as the star of the hit '80s TV show "The Facts of Life." Now that she's the mother of three, Lisa Whelchel has some pertinent thoughts for parents who struggle with disciplining their children. *Creative Correction* draws from her own successes and mistakes to help other parents deal with sibling rivalry, lying and other behavioral challenges. Her creative, down-to-earth encouragement and biblical perspective provide a breath of fresh air to overwhelmed parents everywhere. Hardcover.

Your Child Membership Program

This membership offers parents with children 12 and under age-customized parenting tips, fun activities and more through newsletters, audio journals and Web site features. Visit us at www.focusonyourchild.com and sign up for your membership. (Available in the U.S. only)

Look for these special resources in your Christian bookstore or request an item by calling 1-800-A-FAMILY (1-800-232-6459). Friends in Canada may write to Focus on the Family, P.O. Box 9800, Stn. Terminal, Vancouver, B.C. V6B 4G3 or call 1-800-661-9800.

Visit our Web site (www.family.org) to learn more about the ministry or to find out if there is a Focus on the Family office in your country.

Dr. Dennis W. Swanberg
"America's Minister of Encouragement"
Baylor University 1976, B.A. Religion/Greek
Southwestern Seminary 1980/1986, M.Div.
and Doctor of Ministry

National TV Host of:
"Swan's Place"—FamNet Networks
and
"The Dennis Swanberg Show"—TBN, Saturdays
at 2:30 P.M. CST

National and international
speaker/author/Christian entertainer

Booking and product information:
Swanberg Ministries
P.O. Box 1495
West Monroe, La. 71294
318/325-9044 (office)
318/325-0012 (fax)
www.dennisswanberg.com

Management:
Ron Smith, Smith Management
615/687-6836

p. 75 Classroom needs

p. 94 Impetuous behaviour = disorder

p. 135 parenting & drugs approaches

p. 155 resource

p. 102 ADHD in children
inattentive, easy distractability,
mood swings, quick tempers,
impulsivity, restlessness, irritability,
disorganization

p. 108 impulse control

p. 113 - Symptoms
distractibility is
key